Which School ? for Special Needs 1992/3

GABBITAS
TRUMAN
AND
THRING

Editor: Derek Bingham

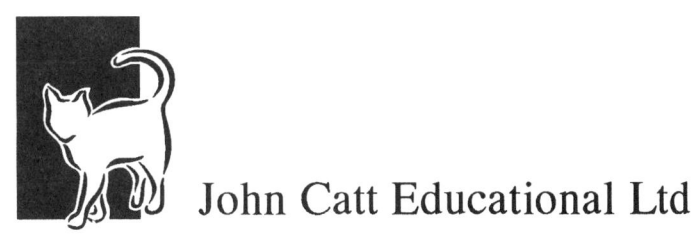

John Catt Educational Ltd

How to use this Guide

by The Editor

Welcome to **Which School ? For Special Needs,** in which we aim to provide as much information as possible about the choices available to parents of children who have Special Educational Needs.

The Guide is divided into five main sections. The first contains editorial articles, written by experts in their fields, explaining aspects of providing education for those with special educational needs, as well as the legal rights of both pupil and parent. We urge you to read them.

The remaining four sections provide information about the schools and colleges which may be able to help you. Details of what each section contains appear in the Contents.

Each of the first three sections after the editorials is divided into two. The first comprises the Directory, which provides basic information about every institution which falls within its section.

The second part is the Listings, which provide a much more comprehensive description of the schools and colleges concerned. Each Directory presents schools in geographical order by county. Listings present schools in alphabetical order. Following the fifth section there is a list of useful associations which can offer advice and help.

At the back is the Index of all institutions which appear in the book. The letter D preceding each page number indicates where a school or college appears in the Directory. A second figure shows where it may be found among the Listings.

There are many ways to use this book to best advantage. If you seek a school in a certain area, look first at the appropriate Directory. It will give you the basic information about all the schools or colleges which may be able to help you.

After you have selected those which may be suitable, look and see if they have taken a Listing. This will provide you with much more information about them before you make a direct approach.

If you know of a school, but are not sure where it is located, turn to the Index. From it you will find the information you want.

Hopefully when you have used this book you will have found a selection of suitable schools of colleges - and even options you had not been previously aware of.

Great Glemham, 1992

Contents

Introduction, *John Murrell MA*	1
Overview: Special Education in the UK, *Peter Kendall BA, PGCE, AFBPsS*	2
Classifying Special Needs, *Dr Susan Ellen Mann BS, MA, EdD, CPsychol*	4
What is Assessment?	12
The role of the Educational Psychologist	16
Choosing a suitable school, *John Fish*	18
Placement: What the law says	22
Glossary of Abbreviations	26
Directory of Schools and Colleges specialising in Sensory or Physical Impairment	27
Display Listings of Schools	37
Display Listings of Colleges of Further Education	57
Directory of Schools specialising in Learning Difficulties	61
Display Listings of Schools specialising in Learning Difficulties	70

Directory of Schools specialising in Emotional and
    Behavioural Difficulties   83

Display Listings of Schools specialising in Emotional and
    Behavioural Difficulties   93

Display Listings of normal curriculum Schools and Colleges
    offering Learning Support   106

Display Listings of Colleges of Further Education
    offering Learning Support   119

Useful Associations   121

Map   136

Index   137

Introduction

by John Murrell, MA, *Senior Managing Governor, Gabbitas, Truman & Thring Educational Trust*

Much work has been done of recent years in classifying the handicaps which some children suffer, and identifying the resources, equipment and teaching methods necessary to overcome them. Gone are the days when children could simply be categorised as 'maladjusted' or 'educationally sub-normal' and sent to a special school accordingly. Things are seldom that simple. It is not sufficient to treat the obvious symptoms: one must find the underlying cause. The shy child who makes no progress at school, not because he is stupid, but because he can't bear the teacher; the tearaway whose uncontrolled behaviour comes from frustration because his dyslexia prevents him from expressing himself.

But the parents of such a child get frustrated too. They know something is wrong, but are fobbed off by platitudes from the school, or entangled by the red tape of a long drawn out statementing process.

Which School ? For Special Needs has been written for the parent. It tries to explain in layman's terms what is meant by special education; how a child's special needs are identified, classified and provided for. It gives information about many schools which can provide the necessary help, and how parents can contact them.

The Gabbitas, Truman & Thring Educational Trust was founded in 1987 by the amalgamation of the two leading educational agencies, Gabbitas-Thring (founded 1873) and Truman & Knightley (founded 1901). It is a non-profit making organisation, and a registered educational charity, dedicated to providing consultancy services to parents. On behalf of the publishers, John Catt Educational Ltd, I should like to express appreciation for the support and contributions we have received and without which publication would not have been possible. I acknowledge with thanks the articles introducing the Guide by Dr Judith Haynes, PhD, FBPsS and Peter Kendall, BA, PGCE, AFBPsS of Child Consultants, Dr Maurice Tyerman, BA, PhD, TCert, C Psychol, FBPsS, Dr Susan Mann, Ed D and John Fish, a former Senior HMI with special responsibility for Special Needs.

But most of all I must thank the individual schools, colleges and institutions who have borne with us as we have prepared the relevant and up-to-date information which is the purpose of this Guide.

Overview: Special Education in the UK

by Peter Kendall, BA, PGCE, AFBPsS,
Director, Child Consultants,

The UK has always had a strong tradition of parental pressure groups leading the way for special provision in education. Special schools were set up by charities such as the Spastics Society, the Invalid Childrens Aid Association and the RNIB, many years before the 1944 Education Act gave impetus to this movement.

Although the Act is rightly remembered for its provision of education for all according to 'age, aptitude and ability', it also empowered local education authorities (LEAs) to spend money for the first time specifically on providing for a variety of handicaps.

The independent special schools tended to be boarding ones with pupils funded by LEAs who then started their own building programmes. These concentrated on establishing day schools for children with moderate learning difficulties, a group which still forms the majority of the special school population, and this development reached its peak in the early 1970s.

Since then, there has been a shift in emphasis from segregation to integration. Mary Warnock's report into how 'handicapped' children were educated led to the 1981 Education Act which substituted the term 'special education needs' (SEN) for 'handicaps'.

The 1981 Act laid on LEAs a duty to identify, assess and educate children with such needs and gave parents an integral part in the assessment process. It was estimated that 18-20% of the school population might have special educational needs at some time or other in their school career, but that a much smaller proportion would require a formal assessment leading to a 'Statement'. This Statement was intended to be a comprehensive list of the child's special educational needs together with details of the provision to meet them.

The main emphasis on provision was to enable mainstream schools to cater for special needs with varying degrees of support. Only when the education of other children was adversely affected or resources were not used efficiently was consideration given to placement in a special school.

One of the results of the 1981 Act was that LEAs switched some of their resources from funding boarding special school places to setting up units in their own mainstream schools. These units would cater in primary schools for less extreme special needs, for instance, partially hearing, delayed speech, moderate learning difficulties, whilst secondary schools would all have their special needs departments.

Recent figures from the Department of Education and Science give the following estimates (all percentages are proportions of the total school population):

* Some 20% have special educational needs.
* 2% are Statemented, made up of:
* 1½% in special schools, and
* ½% in ordinary schools.

About half of the children in special schools fall in the moderate learning difficulty category (MLD), a quarter in the severe learning difficulty range (SLD), and the rest comprise the remaining groups of which emotional and behavioural difficulty (EBD) is the largest. Over the last few years the special school population has remained constant, but the proportion of EBD children has risen. There has been a noticeable increase in Statemented children with the extra numbers being placed almost entirely in ordinary schools.

Special education in the UK has now reached a watershed. On the one hand the policy of integration has reduced the demand for special school places, and the cost of boarding has added to this downward pressure. On the other, the same policy has put an increasing strain on ordinary LEA schools who are now having to manage their own budgets with limited resources for special needs.

Parents are becoming disenchanted with the way some LEAs are interpreting the 1981 Act, and they are again exerting their influence in trying to get the best possible provision for their children. Solicitors specialising in the law relating to special needs are increasingly being consulted by parents, as are groups of independent educational psychologists who can provide unbiased assessments for appeals tribunals and judicial reviews.

The independent sector has always been in the forefront of developments in education. Special needs are again at the top of the agenda, and the schools which combine high quality all-round teaching with good specialist provision will always be in demand. When a child's future is at stake, nothing but the best will do.

Classifying Special Needs

by Dr Susan Ellen Mann, BS, MA, EdD, CPsychol,
Educational psychologist specialising in specific learning difficulties

Children with special needs are different in some significant way from others of the same age. For these children to develop to their full adult potential, their education must be adapted to those differences. Children are considered educationally exceptional only when it is necessary to alter the educational programme: if their exceptionality leaves them unable to read or to master learning in the traditional fashion. In education, we group children of like characteristics for teaching purposes. For example, we put six-year-olds together in a class. In the same way, and for the same reasons, we group children with special needs. The following groups are typical:

Intellectual differences, including children who are intellectually superior and children who are slow to learn.

Sensory differences, including children with auditory or visual impairments.

Communication differences, including children with learning disabilities (dyslexia), or speech and languages impairments.

Behavioural differences, including children who are emotionally disturbed or socially maladjusted.

Physical differences, including children with non-sensory handicaps that impede mobility and physical vitality.

Multiple and severe problems, including children with combinations of impairments (cerebral palsy and mental retardation, deafness and blindness).

Often a special learning environment is necessary to help children with special needs master particular content and skills. Whenever possible we try to keep children with special needs in mainstream regular classrooms. To help the classroom teachers understand the special needs of these children and ways to help them learn effectively, special teachers, consultants could be provided. Speech-language pathologists, social workers, school psychologists, remedial reading teachers, and learning disability specialists may deal with children with special needs and classroom teachers on a consultant basis. This means that youngsters spend most of their time in the regular classroom, and are taken out of the classroom only for short periods of tutorial or remedial help.

Part-time special classes accept children who require more time for special instruction than the short period spent in a resource room. The programmes for the children in these classes are the responsibility of a special class teacher. Children in part-time special classes may spend half a day in special class and the other half in the regular classroom, in subjects in which they can compete.

At times moderately and severely handicapped children learn more effectively in self-contained special classes, where the special education teacher assumes primary responsibility for their programmes. In the past this kind of class was the most common for all exceptional children. Today it has been largely replaced, especially for mildly handicapped students, by visiting special education teachers and part-time special classes.

Some areas have day schools for different kinds of exceptional students, especially those who are behaviourally disturbed, orthopaedically handicapped, moderately mentally retarded and multiply handicapped. In line with the policy of mainstreaming, there are fewer special schools today. Children with mild handicaps can adapt to the regular classrooms.

You may want to get advice on organisations and people able to help you with your child's special educational needs, and local issues. Parents of children aged under five who may have special educational needs should be told by the health authority about any organisation which may be able to provide advice and information. For parents of children with Statements, education authorities must provide the name of a person 'to whom (s)he may apply for information and advice about the child's special educational needs'. Parents are likely to want to seek independent advice and help from the earliest moment. Your local education authority, social services department, district health authority or a Citizen's Advice Bureau may be able to supply parents with information on local groups concerned with specific disability.

Blindness and Visual Impairment

About one child in ten enters school with some degree of visual impairment. Fortunately, most of these problems can be corrected and have little or no effect on social or educational development. But for one in a thousand children, visual impairments are so severe that they can not be corrected. These children are visually handicapped. In general the term 'visually handicapped' is used to describe all degrees of visual impairment - a continuum from severe visual impairment to total blindness.

We use two basic classifications for students who are visually impaired: those who are blind have light perception without projection or are totally without light perception, and must use braille to learn; those with low vision who are severely impaired even with glasses but can read print. Common types of visual disorders are refractive errors, defects of muscle function and other anomalies. Studies on the impact of visual impairment indicate that, in general, intellectual abilities are not markedly affected; the perception of other senses is not different from that of seeing persons, language development is affected only in those areas where the meanings of words are dependent on visual concepts; and self-esteem and self-confidence are not distorted except when a peer group has negatively influenced the individual's attitude.

The many needs of visually impaired children demand a continuum of special services: pre-school programmes, teacher consultants, itinerant teachers, special classes, and special school programmes. Visually impaired children are now attending regular classes whenever possible, using the services of peripatetic teachers to assist them with their special needs.

Deafness and Hearing Impairment

Deaf and hard of hearing children are not a homogeneous group. The degree of hearing loss, the cause of loss, the age at which it was acquired, the type of loss, all combine to make each child's condition unique. A hearing loss interferes with the reception and production of language. Because language influences practically every dimension of human development, the inability to hear or speak intelligibly is a critical handicap that can have enormous social and academic consequences.

Children with hearing losses fall into two major categories: hard of hearing and deaf. With sound amplification the hard of hearing child can understand speech; the deaf child cannot. Prelingual deafness is the loss of hearing before speech and language develop; postlingual deafness is the loss of hearing after speech and language develop. The child who is prelingually deaf faces the most serious learning problems. A conductive hearing loss reduces the intensity of sound reaching the inner ear. A sensorineural hearing loss is caused by a defect of the inner ear or auditory nerve. Conductive losses can be reduced through sound amplification; sensorineural losses cannot.

Recent studies show that deaf children are not cognitively deficient. Their poor cognitive and academic performance may actually stem from their difficulty reading and writing the English language. Because deaf children do not understand the concept of language or complex syntactic structures, they have difficulty reading and writing the English language. The social adjustment of deaf youngsters can be impeded by the difficulty of communication and the behaviours that evolve from their inability to communicate. During the developmental years we must accept that sign language has a positive effect on academic performance and adjustment. The total communication method is the most popular form used to teach deaf children. The teaching of deaf students should include both manual and oral instruction to allow these children to reach their potential.

Physical Disabilities

One of the smallest but most diverse groups of special needs children is the group classified as physically handicapped. Some physical handicaps are obvious, others are subtle. Some are caused by disease, others by injury. Most are permanent. Although most conditions are unrelated they are usually grouped into two categories: physical disabilities or health impairments. A physical disability results from a condition like cerebral palsy or a spinal cord injury that interferes with the child's ability to use his or her body.

Many, but not all, physical disabilities are considered orthopaedic impairments. The term orthopaedic impairment refers to conditions of the muscular or skeletal system, and sometimes to physically disabling conditions of the nervous system. A condition such as cystic fibrosis or diabetes that requires ongoing medical attention is a health impairment. Children with cardiopulmonary conditions have breathing or heart problems that limit participation in physical activities. Children with musculoskeletal conditions have motor skill deficits that in severe cases prevent walking and sitting up. Children with neurological conditions suffer from a range of motor disabilites, from mild incoordination to total paralysis, and sometimes intellectual deficiencies that complicate their development. A physical impairment is not a handicap unless it limits the individual's participation in routine activities.

Children with physical handicaps show a wide range of reactions to their condition. Those with congenital physical handicaps tend to make necessary adaptations to their conditions. Children whose handicaps are caused by injury generally go through a period of mourning before they finally accept and adjust to their conditions. Children whose conditions are caused by disease have the same adjustment problems of other physically handicapped youngsters but also face uncertainty and the academic pressure that stems from frequent absences. Teachers can help students with physical handicaps by adapting the course and learning environment to individual needs. For example, by widening the aisles in the classroom to accommodate a wheelchair, the teacher can reduce the impact of the handicap on the student.

Physically handicapped children, like other special needs children, should be taught in the least restrictive environment. For most of these children this means the regular classroom with extra attention with a peripatetic teacher, if needed. The implementation of the educational programme for children with physical handicaps often includes physical therapists, school nurses, and occupational therapists. These therapists should work in close cooperation with the classroom teacher, to reinforce skill learning. For some children, special schools or homebound or hospital services are essential to their educational programme.

Communication Disorders and Speech Defects

Over the past decades, the field of communication disorders has been expanded to include hearing problems and language disorders as well as speech problems. A child is language impaired when his or her skills in the primary language are markedly below those expected for the child's chronological age. Impaired speech is characterised as being conspicuous, unintelligible and unpleasant. Communication disorders are impairments in articulation, language, voice or fluency. There are five dimensions in language: phonology (sound), morphology (word structure), syntax (sentence structure), semantics (word meaning) and pragmatics (function). A child can be impaired in any or all of these dimensions.

The physical processes needed to produce sound are respiration, phonation, resonation, and articulation. A breakdown in any of these processes can impair speech production. Articulation disorders involve substitutions, omissions, and distortions. For young children, intervention in the regular classroom is the traditional method of remediation. Older children may require either individual or group sessions with a speech-language pathologist. Fluency disorders (stuttering) can be alleviated temporarily through distraction and other devices. Permanent improvement is more difficult. Treatment involves the teaching of rhythmic stuttering and behaviour therapy. Voice disorders are the result of significant deviations in vocal quality, pitch and loudness. Treatment involves careful diagnosis, removal of the cause, where possible, and negative practice. Most speech and language corrective programmes focus on children with communication deviations - those with mild to moderate articulation or voice problems that are causing adaption difficulties in school.

Learning Disabilities

Learning disabilities afflict a heterogeneous group of children who are not developing or learning normally but who do not fit into the traditional categories of handicapped children. The many definitions of learning disabilities agree on two major points: that an intrinsic psychological or neurological factor is inhibiting or interfering with normal development or academic achievement, and the disability cannot be explained by mental retardation, a sensory handicap, emotional disturbance or lack of opportunity to learn. Underachievement and learning disabilities are not synonymous. Learning disabilities are just one cause of underachievement. There are two kinds of learning disabilities: developmental learning disabilities in attention, memory, perception, thinking and language, and academic learning disabilities in reading, spelling, handwriting, and written expression (dyslexia).

The factors that contribute to an academic learning disability are the conditions that inhibit or interfere with a child's academic progress in school. They include physical conditions, environmental factors, motivational and affective factors, and psychological conditions (developmental learning disabilities). Unlike causes, these contributing factors can usually be remediated.

Three criteria are used to identify learning disabled children: (a) discrepancy between abilities, or between potential and achievement; (b) the absence of mental retardation, a sensory handicap, serious emotional disturbance, or environmental disadvantage; and (c) the need for special education services to remediate their disability. There are four common strategies for remediation: (a) task or skill training, in which the components and sequence of the task or skill to be learned are simplified; (b) process training, remediation of a specific developmental disability or dysfunction; (c) process-task training, where both the first two approaches are integrated, and (d) age appropriate behavioural and cognitive strategies are taught.

Mental Retardation

Mental retardation refers to a significantly subaverage general intellectual functioning existing concurrently with deficits in adaptive behaviour and manifested during the developmental period. Adaptive behaviour is defined as the effectiveness or degree to which individuals meet the standards of personal independence and social responsibility expected for their age and cultural group. Students who score on an intelligence scale between 50-55 to 70 are considered mildly mentally retarded if their social adaptation is also low. Students who score between 35-40 to 50-55 but who are capable of responding to the test are considered moderately retarded. An intelligence score below 35 is considered profound or severe mental retardation.

There are many causes of mental retardation. They include genetic disorders, toxic agents, infectious diseases, and polygenic inheritance. Retarded children have difficulty processing information. For many the problem lies in a poorly developed executive function. This can affect their problem-solving capabilities, and expression. Developmental problems in language acquisition and use, physical abilities, and personal and social characteristics form the basis of special education plans for retarded youngsters. The learning environment in which mildly retarded students are usually placed include regular classrooms, part- or full-time special classes. Moderately retarded children are often found in special classes. A well-organised course of study concentrating upon socialization, prevocational skills and teaching life experiences (the need for social cooperation) in addition to academic subjects is a necessity for this population.

Emotional and Behavioural Difficulties

Few experiences are so disturbing to teachers as encountering children who are chronically unhappy or distressed, or driven to aggressive, antisocial behaviour. It is not easy to define behaviour problems in children. Most definitions assume that children with behaviour problems reveal consistent age-inappropriate behaviour leading to social conflict, personal unhappiness, and school failure. But almost all children reveal age-inappropriate behaviour at one time or another. The definition then, depends on the dimensions of intensity and duration and inappropriateness that schools feel compelled to take special action.

There are four major classifications of problem behaviour: conduct disorders, anxiety-withdrawal, immaturity, and socialised aggression. Identification methods include teacher ratings, self-reports, parent and peer ratings, and behaviour observations. Approaches to modify the educational programmes of children with behavioural differences include drug therapy, behaviour modification, and psychodynamic strategies.

Drug therapy carefully administered under competent supervision can modify hyperactive behaviour when combined with specially designed educational experiences. Behaviour modification techniques have yielded positive, consistent results in achieving specific objectives. One strategy for helping children with behavioural differences has been to focus on the ecological setting; the interaction of children and their environment. Treatment consists of direct counselling as well as efforts to change the surrounding environment, to make it more receptive to these children. Several techniques that teach children to manage their own behaviour seem to help children cope with acting-out behaviour problems. Treatment for withdrawn or depressed children generally focuses on strategies that enable these youngsters to express fears and to improve, through developing competence, and self-esteem.

Severe or multihandicapping conditions include mental retardation combined with cerebral palsy, mental retardation and hearing impairment, mental retardation and severe behaviour problems, autism, behaviour disturbance and hearing impairment, and deaf-blind impairments. Legislative and judicial actions over the last two decades have resulted in a movement to deinstitutionalize and to normalize individuals with severe and multiple handicaps.

The teaching strategies for severely and multiply handicapped students have been influenced by task analysis and operant conditioning. These procedures break down a task into target behaviours and apply the principles of learning to instruction. The curriculum for young children who are severely and multiply handicapped should focus on communication, social development, and prevocational skills development. The curriculum for severely and multiply handicapped adolescents focuses on their ultimate functioning, the degree to which these students are able to actively participate in community situations appropriate to their age level.

The development of educational programmes for those who are severely handicapped requires an analysis of their daily routine, skill assessment, identification of teaching goals and strategies, staff training, and management of the many elements and participants in the programme. Normalisation is an ongoing process. It does not end as the severely handicapped child becomes an adult. An important element in the process is the creation of integrative living arrangements in family or foster homes, group homes, or community residential institutions.

What is assessment?

Informal assessment is an everyday occurrence. All adults and children assess or judge other people by what they say or do and sometimes by how they look.

Parents judge how their child is progressing by noting what he or she can do (criterion reference assessment) and how he compares with other children of his own age (normative reference assessment).

Teachers do the same. As a matter of routine they observe their pupils and record their impressions of their behaviour and their work. They correct and supplement this information from the results of informal tests in class, both oral and written (curriculum based assessment). These also tell them how successful their teaching has been and how they should proceed. Teachers learn much, too, by comparing their impressions with those of parents. They can help each other to help the child.

Teachers tend to record these assessments in two ways: personal notes for their own day-to-day guidance and in more formal reports which can be passed from teacher to teacher throughout the school. If desired these can be incorporated into records of achievement which can be owned by both children and their parents in partnership with the school.

Following the 1988 Education Reform Act the National Curriculum is being gradually introduced into all schools which are publicly maintained. These are county schools which are established and run by local education authorities (LEAs) and voluntary schools which are funded by LEAs but were founded by other bodies, usually religious denominations. However, that Curriculum is not compulsory in independent schools, non-maintained special schools or for certain pupils with Statements in LEA schools, whether special or ordinary.

The National Curriculum describes what children should learn at particular ages (termed key stages) and at 7, 11 and 14 (stages I, II, III and IV respectively) pupils are tested by standard assessment tasks (SATS) to see how far they have reached them. At the same time the child's teacher makes her own assessments of each pupil's progress and the two types of evidence are combined for each subject. This new procedure will doubtlessly undergo gradual changes as a result of experience.

Increasingly, teachers' own tests will become more and more linked to the demands of the National Curriculum and the results, like those of the SATS, expressed in terms of levels (one of four) and stages.

Some independent schools formally assess pupils who are seeking places in the school. They often use published tests, particularly at 11 and 13 (Common Entrance) to help them judge whether candidates' learning ability and the standards they have reached will enable them to fit easily into the life of the schools to which they are applying and to profit from their teaching. They usually supplement such assessments by reports from pupils' present schools.

Statutory Assessment

Boys and girls who have difficulties need special consideration whatever those difficulties might be. Only in that way can they be helped to do their best. But first they must be recognised as being in need, the nature of their difficulties explored, decisions reached as to what should be done to overcome or mitigate whatever is holding them back and what arrangements should be made to provide them with whatever assistance is required.

For children whose difficulties are severe, one way of doing this is through a statutory examination or assessment under the Education Act 1981. This can lead to a Statement being made of difficulties, special educational needs (SEN) and the measures which are proposed to meet them. The LEA is legally obliged to find out and supply what the child with SEN requires unless the child's parents or guardians have made alternative arrangements for education and will be responsible for the fees.

Under the 1981 Education Act a pupil is considered to have SEN if he or she has a 'learning difficulty' which calls for special educational provision to be made. Such provision would be additional to, or different from, that which is generally available to children in ordinary classes in the LEA. This situation will usually become apparent during the child's first or second year in school.

Such a pupil will either have significantly greater difficulties in learning than the majority of children of the same age and/or have a disability which prevents him or her from making effective use of the facilities of the local school. If the child is under five the LEA must consider whether he would be likely to encounter either of those situations if special educational arrangements were not made.

If the young child's disabilities are severe, parents will probably have been working closely with the local medical services from an early age. The District Health Authority (DHA) will usually have alerted the LEA and the Social Services Departments (SSD) so that suitable help for the parents and directly to the child might be given as soon as possible.

In some cases a visiting teacher might come regularly to the child's home and/or a place be made available in a playgroup or **nursery** type school, part-time, full-time, or even residential if necessary. The actual nature of the help offered will, to some extent, be determined by what is available in the area and above all by the parents' wishes.

About two per cent of children have difficulties which require them to be given long-term assistance through the protection of a Statement. Approximately another 18% of pupils are generally thought to need some extra help some of the time; usually they are not given Statements.

Learning difficulties may arise from physical causes, for example impaired sight or hearing, or from limited intellectual ability. Often there are emotional or social reasons where too much of a child's energies are directed to coping with personal stress or unhappiness to enable him to concentrate on schoolwork or even to conform to the demands of school routine.

The Education Act 1981, and subsequent circulars issued by the DES, define how the examination, or more accurately examinations and reports which can lead to a Statement under Section 5 of the 1981 Act, are to be carried out.

The parents must be told when the LEA considers that an examination which may lead to a Statement appears necessary and they must be helped, if they so wish, to object to it. This should not be the first time that they are made aware by the school, or by the LEA, of the child's difficulties.

In making the assessment and deciding what help the pupil requires, the key figures are the head of the child's school, a medical officer of the DHA and the LEA's educational psychologist. Their reports should be supplemented by anyone who has particular skills or additional knowledge of the child's situation and how best he can be helped. These may include specialist teachers, home teachers, speech therapists, physiotherapists, social service officers, family doctors, paediatricians and psychiatrists.

Above all in these judgements are the opinions and wishes of the parents or guardians derived from their intimate knowledge of the child, his development and feelings. In education generally, and especially in the assessment and education of children with SEN, parents should be seen as partners of the school and of the LEA. At all stages they must be involved and kept informed.

Following the examinations the Statement, with any supporting documents, must first of all be given to the child's mother and father in draft and their comments invited. There are various appeals procedures to resolve any differences of opinion between the parents and the LEA.

The Statement should provide a summary of what the child can do, cannot do, and what he is expected to achieve both in the short and long terms in education and personal development. Whatever SEN is described in the Statement, the LEA is legally bound to meet. It must describe the type of school it considers appropriate for the child and name a particular school, if one is known. If appropriate, it must also say how he is to be educated if not at a school.

For a child with a Statement there must be, by law, at least once a year, a review of progress and the suitability of the school attended. The LEA usually undertakes this through reports from school.

In addition there must be a full statutory examination when a child is aged between 13½ and 14½ if his previous statutory examination had taken place before he was 12½ years old. There should also be a repeat statutory examination when the pupil's mother and father reasonably so wish or when changes in the child's circumstances indicate that one is required. In all these examinations the child's view must be sought and considered. He must be helped to contribute in the decision about what is best for him and this will often include visiting the school that is proposed.

Which type of school - an ordinary school must be considered first - and which particular school is most appropriate will obviously depend on the child's difficulties, personality, the way of life needed and the facilities of the schools available.

Where a child has SEN but no Statement, the LEA must act with certain reservations in accord with parental preferences.

Independent schools, non-maintained schools and hospital schools are not required to follow the National Curriculum. In those which do, the Statements of certain pupils may have altered or removed some or all of the demands of the National Curriculum if these are inappropriate for the children concerned. A boy or girl awaiting formal assessment may also be similarly excused. But the LEA must substitute some appropriate provision in their stead in order to maintain a balanced and broadly based curriculum for that particular child.

The provisions of the 1981 Act apply from birth to age 16. But children aged 16 who have Statements may stay at school if they so wish until they are 19 years of age and the LEA may help them.

They may also be assisted to attend day or residential colleges of further education. LEAs have considerable discretion in the aid which they can give.

The Role of the Educational Psychologist

by Peter Kendall, BA, PGCE, AFBPsS,
Director, Child Consultants

Educational psychologists have a central role in assessment. They are required to provide evidence of how a child is functioning and what precisely are its special educational needs, and to write a detailed description of what educational provision would meet those needs.

To assess how children function the educational psychologist draws on a variety of training and experience: training as a teacher followed by practice in the classroom, qualification in psychology and further training and practice as an educational psychologist. Good psychologists add their own personal experience, often as parents, to illuminate what difficulties a child may be having and how best to resolve them.

Children function in different ways intellectually, socially, emotionally and academically, and an assessment should take account of all these factors. We know that intelligence has a bearing on school success. The more intelligent a child, the quicker the rate of learning, the more retentive the memory and the more complex the material that can be absorbed. Intelligence tests, sensitively applied, can be a good guide as to what to expect. Results can highlight children who are underfunctioning as well as those of whom too much is being expected.

Emotional and social development is harder to measure but has a considerable impact on how children learn in school. Some may be stuck at an earlier stage, and whilst having the mental ability to do well are prevented from doing so by immaturity. Social skills smooth the way for a child in new settings - starting school, moving up a form, changing teachers - and those who have not acquired the knack of making friends find life much more difficult.

Personality is also difficult to quantify but has a great effect. Everyone recognises the self-confident child who is not afraid of tackling something new. Conversely, children who are over-cautious and timid have more problems in making a success of school. The psychologist can help decide which factors are having the most influence on progress.

Academic achievement can be assessed in younger children by measuring their progress in literacy and numeracy. Being able to read and write fluently, and feeling confident in handling numbers gives any child a head start in education. The psychologist can use accurate tests of reading, spelling and mathematics to detect any gaps and possible specific learning difficulties.

Older children may have academic problems of a more subtle kind: studying effectively, organising their ideas and remembering efficiently. Here again, the educational psychologist can identify weak areas and suggest action.

Most educational psychologists are employed by local education authorities and have a difficult task maintaining their professional independence. On the one hand they are employees whose paymasters have limited resources for special needs and definite policies on integration. On the other, they have a primary responsibility to identify the needs of the child to the best of their ability, and to specify the provision required without fear or favour. Parents can help maintain the standards of assessments by taking an active role in the process. They need to become more knowledgeable about their rights under the Education Act 1981, to insist on detailed and thorough investigations, and to obtain independent advice whenever they feel their child's needs are taking second place. In this way we can all play a part in ensuring that every child with special needs obtains the quality of assessment and provision to which they are entitled.

Choosing a suitable school

by John Fish, *Educational Consultant, formerly HMI*

Choosing a school for a child who has a disability or learning difficulty is often a problem. Two aspects of the process have to be considered together. They are assessment of a child's needs and how they should be met; and a school's ability to provide for children with special educational needs.

Nobody knows better than parents that their children's special educational needs are individual to them. Children with the same degree of hearing loss or learning difficulty, for example, do not have the same needs. In the same way schools providing for the same type of special need vary.

Choice is always difficult but it is made easier by being well informed about what is available. This article sets out some of the information you may need.

A child's assessed needs

In order to start the process of choice these questions have to be asked and answered:

Have your child's special educational needs been assessed?

Have they been assessed privately by doctors and psychologists?

Have they been assessed by the local education authority?

Is your child the subject of a Statement?

The answers can then lead to questions about schools.

Assessing school provision

There are three ways in which independent schools may make provision for children with special educational needs. These are:

Independent schools, providing a standard curriculum, which have no special provision but which are sensitive to individual variations in learning ability.

Schools which have special arrangements for particular groups, for example children with specific learning difficulties.

Schools approved by the Secretary of State for children who are the subject of Statements of their special educational needs.

Schools vary in the ways in which they are inspected and approved. There are what are known as general inspection procedures which apply to all schools and there are specific approval procedures for particular groups of schools.

General inspection

All schools are liable to inspection as directed by the Secretary of State for Education and Science. These inspections will comment on the quality of any special educational provision made by schools. The Children Act 1989 has made Local Authority Social Service Departments responsible for the inspection of child care arrangements in all boarding schools including independent schools. Implemented in October 1991 it will take some time for authorities to have any detailed knowledge of schools.

HM Inspections look at teaching staff qualifications and proficiency, educational and residential accommodation, the curriculum and how it is delivered and the general care and welfare of pupils. HM Inspectorate reports are published and parents can obtain them. At the time of writing inspection arrangements for schools are the subject of new legislation.

Specific procedures

Some independent schools also have to reach certain standards set by the associations of which they are members, for example the IAPS. At present there is no specific assessment or endorsement by those associations of provision made for pupils with disabilities and learning difficulties. The extent to which City Technology Colleges and Grant Maintained Schools make special educational provision is a matter for local enquiry. At present there is a requirement to include such needs in planning but no evidence of the extent to which provision is being made.

Special Education

In addition to special schools maintained by local education authorities there are two other kinds of school catering wholly or mainly for children with special educational needs, non-maintained special schools and approved independent schools. Both are inspected by HMI. The 1981 Education Act makes the inspection and approval of such independent schools a necessity if children who are the subject of Statements are to be placed in them by local education authorities.

There is also an association of independent special schools, the National Association of Independent and Non-Maintained Special Schools (see page 121), which sets standards for membership. Parents can consult that association.

Matching schools and needs

There are again two stages. The first step is to look at the answers to the questions about assessment. They help to identify the kind of school which might be appropriate.

Question 1 If your child *has been* assessed, the kind of school you may choose depends on answers to questions 2 and 3. If your child *has not been* assessed there are two courses open to you. You may prefer to rely on your own judgement of your child's educational needs, or you may seek assessment. If you take the first course you should follow the general guidance for selecting any school and in addition look at how the school deals with individual differences in the ways and rates at which children learn.

Question 2 If your child *has been assessed independently,* then the persons carrying out the assessment may have some recommendations to make about appropriate schools. If not you can consult an appropriate voluntary organisation or parents' group such as MENCAP or the Dyslexia Association or an appropriate association of independent schools.

Question 3 If your child *has been assessed by the local education authority,* your child may or may not be the subject of a Statement. Parents have a right to be informed at all stages of the assessment process and thus should know whether their child has special educational needs or not, and is or is not the subject of a Statement. If your child *is not the subject of a Statement* you have the same choice of schools as other parents. However, you will need to find out what provision schools make for special educational needs.

If your child *has been made the subject of a Statement* then the local education authority is responsible for making provision. Your child should only attend a maintained or non-maintained special school or an independent school approved for children with Statements of special educational needs under the 1981 Education Act.

What should parents look for?

All schools should include information about the arrangements they make for pupils with special educational needs in their prospectus. All are inspected and HMI reports should be made available. Local education authorities also look very closely at the non-maintained and independent schools they use and this may be a guide to choice.

Given this information parents should then make a short list of a small number of schools, which appear to have good reports, are members of a reputable association of independent schools and which they think might suit their child, and arrange to visit them.

In addition to the information you would seek from any school, particular questions should be asked about staff qualifications and experience with the particular special educational need of the child, what professional support the staff receive from appropriate health, therapeutic and psychological services and whether the same standards are expected of pupils with special needs. It does not help these children if standards and expectations are low.

It is particularly important to ask secondary schools about post-school opportunities for children with special needs. Links with further and higher education are vital as are expectations that children with disabilities will have career prospects. All too often there is little planning for post-school provision.

Conclusions

The choice of a school is often one of the most difficult parental responsibilities. Schools change, inspections are seldom recent and school reputations are based on those who leave. In addition parents of children with disabilities and learning difficulties are expected to make their way through a maze of different professional opinions and responsibilities for meeting their children's needs. Changing legislation and increased independence for individual schools is making things no easier for them.

It is to be hoped that the independent sector will, in future, provide more information to parents not only about the provision made for pupils with disabilities and learning difficulties but also about the standards of that provision. Meanwhile this guidance is offered as an interim solution.

Placement: What the law says

An LEA must, by law, consider, both initially and at a review, whether a child's SEN can be met in an ordinary school, perhaps with some special arrangements being made, before recommending a special school. The LEA can specify and provide any non-educational facilities considered advisable.

Special schools outside LEA provision fall into two main categories: independent or private schools and non-maintained schools. The principal difference is that non-maintained schools are non profit making though that is also true of certain independent schools which have charitable purposes. Both independent and non-maintained schools may be for boarding (in some cases 52 weeks a year) or for day pupils or both and be single sex or co-educational.

Independent schools are of two types, those which have been approved and those which have not. Approval may have been withheld or it may not have been sought.

LEAs are able to place pupils in independent special schools which have been approved by the Secretary of State as being suitable for pupils with particular specified difficulties or disorders. The DES list of such schools is subject to revision as schools close or change in various ways and new schools open. The LEA cannot place a child with a particular type of need in an independent school which has been approved as suitable for pupils with a different type of need. Nor can a child be placed there if admission would alter the conditions under which the school was approved, for example an older child being placed in a school which has been approved for younger children.

The approval of an independent school depends on satisfactory reports from the school, HMI and various local authority officials but it is primarily the responsibility of an LEA which is placing a child to keep under review the quality of the education and the childcare arrangements which the school offers to each individual child they have placed there. Schools must enable representatives of LEAs and the Social Services Department to visit at all reasonable times and to inspect the school and its records.

The school should have a complaints procedure which is described in writing and given to pupils so that they can raise matters which cannot be dealt with informally.

If the LEA considers that a particular school which has not been approved is the most suitable available for a particular boy or girl it must seek the Secretary of State's consent before transferring a child there.

However, the Secretary of State's agreement is not required if a child without a Statement is placed by parents, for assessment purposes, at an un-approved independent school but his permission must be obtained if, after the assessment, the LEA wishes the pupil to stay there.

His consent is also not needed if parents, guardians or the SSD privately place a child with a Statement at a school which has not been approved. However, if the LEA later takes over responsibility for that child then the Secretary of State's permission is required.

Some unapproved independent special schools are required to register as children's homes if they have 50 or fewer boarders.

Non-maintained special schools are dealt with under a separate legislative framework from independent special schools.

As with independent schools, a non-maintained school may be day or boarding or both and be single sex or co-educational. Many of them were set up to educate pupils with a particular physical disability. They tend therefore to have a wide range of support services and to pay considerable regard to the requirements of adult living and the preparation for it.

Sixteen charitable institutions, some of them internationally known, founded the non-maintained schools but their major income is now from fees paid by LEAs. However, some may also receive grants from central government for capital expenditure.

The Secretary of State has recently updated guidance to non-maintained special schools, particularly in relation to their governing bodies and details of the information which they should give to the DES.

The governors of a non-maintained special school are held responsible in law for the education and social welfare of its pupils and like independent special schools must have regard to the provisions of the Children Act of 1989 as well as those of the Education Acts of 1944 and 1981 and other relevant enactments. Governors usually delegate much of the day to day control of the school to the Head.

The Secretary of State can require governors to be chosen from representatives of parents, teachers and LEAs. However since most non-maintained schools are regulated by trusts and, in accordance with trust law, teachers as employees should not be involved in the management of the trust, there has to be some separation of responsibilities for management from those relating to the day to day running of the school to enable teachers' representatives to play their proper part.

Non-maintained special schools must prepare and publish, before each school year, a prospectus which gives information about the school for the coming year and send copies to the DES and, if requested, to parents and to LEAs who maintain children at the school. They must also send to the DES any additional information which may be required.

If the school wishes to change the special educational needs for which it caters, alter pupil numbers or to admit other types of pupil, it must seek permission. Non-maintained special schools must also follow the regulations which cover the standards required for medical accommodation and sickrooms as well as for the safety and protection of the pupils. Generally their premises must be at least as good as those of maintained special schools.

Non-maintained schools are not obliged to follow the National Curriculum but the Secretary of State expects that many of them will do so. They must therefore make arrangements with the placing LEA about any exceptions to the National Curriculum for any particular child and, if so requested, give the LEA details about the curriculum he will follow. They are expected, as are all schools, to keep records of the progress through the curriculum of all pupils and to revise such records annually.

CHiLD CONSULTANTS

*For a Professional approach to
Assessment & Guidance in Education*

Our services range from tests which you can give your child at home to detailed interviews and assessments by one of our Chartered Psychologists.

We can assess intelligence, monitor academic progress and in this way help you to make informed decisions about your child's schooling.

We have extensive experience of the 1981 Education Act and its implications for children undergoing formal assessment leading to a statement. We can advise on appropriate courses of action even in cases where children have been assessed elsewhere.

For a free brochure, write or telephone us at:

Child Consultants
3 Devonshire Court
26a Devonshire Street
London W1N 1RJ
Telephone: 071-935 9659

Glossary of Abbreviations

AUT	Autism
Bl	Blind Pupils
CP	Cerebral Palsy
D	Deaf Pupils
DYS	Dyslexia
EBD	Emotional/behavioural difficulties
EPI	Epilepsy
MH	Mental Handicap
MLD	Moderate Learning Difficulties
PH	Physical Handicap
PHe	Partial Hearing
SLD	Severe Learning Difficulties
SMH	Severe Mental Handicap
SpD	Speech Defect
SpL	Special Learning Difficulties
VIS	Visual Impairment

Directory of Schools and Colleges specialising in Sensory or Physical Impairment

Berkshire

THE MARY HARE GRAMMAR SCHOOL FOR THE DEAF
Arlington Manor, Newbury, Berkshire RG16 9BQ
Tel: (0635) 248303
Head: I G Tucker
Type: Co-educational Boarding & Day 11-19
No of pupils: B90 G97 No of boarders 189
Special Needs: D
Non - maintained

Cheshire

BETHESDA SCHOOL
Schools Hill, Cheadle, Cheshire SK8 1JE
Tel: (061) 428 7897
Head: C Evans
Type: Co-educational Boarding & Day 11-19 *No of pupils:* 48
Special Needs: BI MLD PH SLD SpD
Non - maintained

DELAMERE FOREST SCHOOL
Blakemere Lane, Norley, Frodsham, Warrington, Cheshire WA6 6LS
Tel: (0928) 88263
Head: S Lewis
Type: Co-educational Boarding & Day 6-17
No of pupils: B35 G25 No of boarders 45
Special Needs: DYS EBD MLD PHe SpD SpL VIS
Non - maintained

ROYAL SCHOOL FOR THE DEAF (MANCHESTER)
Stanley Road, Cheadle Hulme, Cheadle, Cheshire SK8 6RF
Tel: (061) 437 5951
Head: B McCracken
Type: Co-educational Boarding & Day 5-20+
No of pupils: B90 G50 No of boarders 100
Special Needs: D EBD MH MLD PH PHe SLD SMH VIS
Non - maintained

Derbyshire

ALDERWASLEY HALL
Whatstandwell, Matlock, Derbyshire DE4 5HR
Tel: (0629) 822586
Head: K Haywood
Type: Co-educational Boarding & Day 5-19
No of pupils: B109 G27 No of boarders 104
Special Needs: D DYS PHe SpD
Approved Independent

CALDWELL HALL
Caldwell, Burton-upon-Trent, Derbyshire DE12 6RS
Tel: (0283) 761352
Head: Mrs B W Brook
Type: Co-educational Boarding & Day 16+
Special Needs: D DYS MLD PH PHe SLD SpD
Approved Independent

COLLEGE FOR DEAF PEOPLE (DERBY)
Ashbourne Road, Derby, DE3 3BH
Tel: (0332) 362512 ext 235
Head: Mrs F Ison-Jacques
Type: Co-educational Boarding 16-27
No of pupils: B28 G40 No of boarders 68
Special Needs: D EBD MH MLD PH PHe SLD SpL VIS
Non - maintained

THE GRANGE
Mickleover, Derby, DE3 5DR
Tel: (0332) 510951
Head: Mrs B W Brook
Type: Co-educational Boarding & Day
Special Needs: D DYS MLD PH PHe SpD SpL
Approved Independent

ROYAL SCHOOL FOR THE DEAF
Ashbourne Road, Derby, DE3 3BH
Tel: (0332) 362512
Head: T Sylvester
Type: Co-educational Boarding & Day 5-16
No of pupils: B44 G41 No of boarders 38
Special Needs: D PHe
Non - maintained

Devon

DAME HANNAH ROGERS SCHOOL
Ivybridge, Devon PL21 9HQ
Tel: (0752) 892461
Head: W R Evans
Type: Co-educational Boarding & Day 8-19
No of pupils: B25 G25 No of boarders 50
Special Needs: MLD PH PHe SLD SpL VIS
Non - maintained

ROYAL WEST OF ENGLAND SCHOOL FOR THE DEAF
50 Topsham Road, Exeter, Devon EX2 4NF
Tel: (0392) 72692/210842
Head: H P Jones
Type: Co-educational Boarding & Day 3-19
No of pupils: B81 G74 No of boarders 115
Special Needs: D PHe
Non - maintained

TRENGWEATH SCHOOL
Hartley Road, Plymouth, Devon PL3 5LP
Tel: (0752) 771975/773735
Head: Mrs J A Steward
Type: Co-educational Boarding & Day Up ro 12
No of pupils: B15 G11 No of boarders 12
Special Needs: PH PHe SLD SMH SpD SpL VIS
Approved Independent

VRANCH HOUSE SCHOOL & HILL BARTON HOUSE
Pinhoe Road, Exeter, Devon EX4 8AD
Tel: (0392) 68333
Head: S C Johnson
Type: Co-educational Boarding & Day 3-12
No of pupils: 40 No of boarders 12
Special Needs: MLD PH SLD SpD SpL
Approved Independent

THE WEST OF ENGLAND SCHOOL
Countess Wear, Exeter, Devon EX2 6HA
Tel: (0392) 413333
Head: T K Slade
Type: Co-educational Boarding & Day 3-16
Special Needs: BI VIS
Non - maintained

Dorset

LANGSIDE SCHOOL
Parkstone, Poole, Dorset BH12 5BN
Tel: (0202) 518635
Head: Mrs K I Vandervelde
Type: Co-educational Boarding & Day 2-19
No of pupils: B19 G17 No of boarders 5
Special Needs: MH MLD PH PHe SLD SpD SpL VIS
Approved Independent

THE VICTORIA SCHOOL
12 Lindsay Road, Branksome Park, Poole, Dorset BH13 6AS
Tel: (0202) 761473
Head: T C Lane
Type: Co-educational Boarding & Day 3-16
No of pupils: B25 G25 No of boarders 12
Special Needs: MLD PH SpD
Non - maintained

Gloucestershire

THE NATIONAL STAR CENTRE COLLEGE OF FURTHER EDUCATION FOR DISABLED YOUTH
Ullenwood Manor, Cheltenham, Gloucestershire GL53 9QU
Tel: (0242) 527631
Head: A Field
Type: Co-educational Boarding & Day 16+
No of pupils: B60 G60
Special Needs: BI D DYS PH PHe SpD SpL VIS
Approved Independent

ST ROSE'S SPECIAL SCHOOL
Stratford Lawn, Stroud, Gloucestershire GL5 4AB
Tel: (0453) 763793
Head: Sister M Quentin
Type: Co-educational Boarding & Day 2-19
No of pupils: B50 G50 No of boarders 50
Special Needs: BI EPI MLD PH SpD
Non - maintained

Hampshire

LORD MAYOR TRELOAR COLLEGE
Holybourne, Alton, Hampshire GU34 4EN
Tel: (0420) 83508
Head: H Heard
Type: Co-educational Boarding & Day 7-19
No of pupils: B170 G101 No of boarders 246
Special Needs: MLD PH PHe SpD SpL VIS
Non - maintained

MORDAUNT SCHOOL
Rose Road, Southampton, Hampshire SO2 1AE
Tel: (0703) 229017
Head: Miss K Haddaway
Type: Co-educational Day 2-19
No of pupils: 28
Special Needs: BI D MH PH PHe SLD SMH SpD VIS
Approved Independent

Hereford & Worcester

RNIB NEW COLLEGE
Whittington Road, Worcester WR5 2JX
Tel: (0905) 763933
Head: Rev B R Manthorp
Type: Co-educational Boarding & Day 9-19
No of pupils: B78 G40
Special Needs: BI VIS
Non - maintained

ROCHESTER HOUSE
Canon Frame, Ledbury, Hereford & Worcester
Tel: (053183) 670428
Head: Mrs M Norris
Type: Girls Boarding 16+
Special Needs: D PHe

ROYAL NATIONAL COLLEGE FOR THE VISUALLY IMPAIRED
College Road, Hereford HR1 1EB
Tel: (0432) 265725
Head: Rev H M Semple
Type: Co-educational Boarding & Day 16-40
No of pupils: B134 G71 No of boarders 205
Special Needs: BI VIS
Approved Independent

Hertfordshire

MELDRETH MANOR SCHOOL
Meldreth, Royston, Hertfordshire SG8 6LG
Tel: (0763) 260771
Head: C Coles
Type: Co-educational Boarding & Day 8-19
No of pupils: 80 No of boarders 80
Special Needs: D PH SLD VIS
Approved Independent

ST ELIZABETH'S R C SCHOOL
South End, Much Hadham, Hertfordshire SG10 6EW
Tel: (0279) 843451
Head: Sister Veronica Hagen
Type: Co-educational Boarding & Day 5-19
No of pupils: B40 G40 No of boarders 80
Special Needs: EBD EPI MLD PH SLD SpL
Non - maintained

Isle of Wight

ST CATHERINE'S SCHOOL
Grove Road, Ventnor, Isle of Wight PO38 1TT
Tel: (0983) 852722
Head: D G Thomas
Type: Co-educational Boarding & Day 5-16
No of pupils: B36 G12 No of boarders 48
Special Needs: SpD
Non - maintained

Kent

CONEY HILL SCHOOL
Croydon Road, Hayes, Bromley, Kent BR2 7AG
Tel: (081) 462 7419
Head: Mrs D E Hobbs
Type: Co-educational Boarding & Day 5-16
No of pupils: B5 G6 No of boarders 11
Special Needs: MLD PH PHe SLD SpD SpL VIS
Non - maintained

DELARUE COLLEGE
Shipbourne Road, Tonbridge, Kent TN11 9NP
Tel: (0732) 354584
Head: Mrs S M Whalley
Type: Co-educational Boarding & Day 16-19
No of pupils: B15 G14 No of boarders 29
Special Needs: D EBD MH MLD PH PHe SLD SMH SpD SpL VIS
Approved Independent

DORTON HOUSE SCHOOL FOR THE BLIND
Seal, Sevenoaks, Kent TN15 0EB
Tel: (0732) 61477
Head: P J Talbot
Type: Co-educational Boarding & Day 4-16
No of pupils: B54 G57 No of boarders 61
Special Needs: BI MLD VIS
Non - maintained

NASH HOUSE
Croydon Road, Hayes, Bromley, Kent BR2 7AG
Tel: (081) 462 7419
Head: Mrs D E Hobbs
Type: Co-educational Boarding & Day 16-19
No of pupils: B16 G9 No of boarders 25
Special Needs: MLD PH PHe SpD SpL VIS
Non - maintained

THE ROYAL SCHOOL FOR DEAF CHILDREN (MARGATE)
Victoria Road, Margate, Kent CT9 1NB
Tel: (0843) 227561
Head: B S Armstrong
Type: Co-educational Boarding & Day 4-19
No of pupils: B85 G80 No of boarders 165
Special Needs: D
Non - maintained

Lancashire

BIRTENSHAW HALL SCHOOL
Darwen Road, Bromley Cross, Bolton, Lancashire BL7 9AB
Tel: (0204) 54230
Head: C D Jamieson
Type: Co-educational Boarding & Day 3-19
No of pupils: B23 G23 No of boarders 14
Special Needs: MLD PH SLD SpD
Non - maintained

ROYAL CROSS PRIMARY SCHOOL
Elswick Road, Ashton-on-Ribble, Preston, Lancashire PR2 1NT
Tel: (0772) 729705
Head: Mrs P Clancy
Type: Co-educational Day 3-11
No of pupils: B19 G12
Special Needs: D SpL
Non - maintained

Lincolnshire

THE MANOR HOUSE
72 Church Street, Market Deeping, Peterborough, Lincolnshire PE6 8AL
Tel: (0778) 344921
Head: D Ford
Type: Co-educational Boarding 16+
No of pupils: B14 G16 No of boarders 30
Special Needs: BI D MLD PHe SLD VIS
Non - maintained

London

HALLIWICK COLLEGE
Bush Hill Road, London N21 2DU
Tel: (081) 360 2442
Head: Mrs J Durham
Type: Co-educational Boarding & Day 16-30
No of pupils: 50 No of boarders 50
Special Needs: EBD MH MLD PH PHe SLD SpD SpL VIS
Independent

HORNSEY CENTRE FOR CHILDREN LEARNING
26a Dukes Avenue, Muswell Hill, London N10 2PT
Tel: (081) 444 7242
Head: Mrs M L Lilley
Type: Co-educational Day to 7
No of pupils: B3 G5
Special Needs: CP PH
Approved Independent

Merseyside

BIRKDALE SCHOOL FOR HEARING IMPAIRED CHILDREN
40 Lancaster Road, Birkdale, Southport,
Merseyside PR8 2JY
Tel: (0704) 67220
Head: E Loxham
Type: Co-educational Boarding & Day 4-16
No of pupils: B71 G66 No of boarders 86
Special Needs: D
Non - maintained

ROYAL SCHOOL FOR THE BLIND
Wavertree School, Clifton House, Church Road North,
Wavertree, Merseyside
Tel: (051) 733 1012
Head: H S D Marks
Type: Co-educational Boarding & Day 3-19
No of pupils: B25 G25 No of boarders 30
Special Needs: Bl D EBD MLD SLD SpL VIS
Non - maintained

ST VINCENT'S SCHOOL
Yew Tree lane, Merseyside,
Merseyside L12 9HN
Tel: (051) 228 9968
Head: Sister J Hawes
Type: Co-educational Boarding & Day 4-17
No of pupils: B63 G41 No of boarders 57
Special Needs: Bl SpL VIS
Non - maintained

Middlesex

RNIB SUNSHINE HOUSE SCHOOL
33 Dene Road, Northwood,
Middlesex HA6 1DD
Tel: (09274) 22538
Head: Mrs M J Walker
Type: Co-educational Boarding & Day 2-8
No of pupils: B19 G8 No of boarders 6
Special Needs: Bl D EBD MH MLD PH PHe SLD SMH SpD SpL VIS
Non - maintained

Northamptonshire

HINWICK HALL COLLEGE OF FURTHER EDUCATION
Wellingborough, Northamptonshire NN9 7JD
Tel: (0933) 312470
Head: E E Sinnott
Type: Co-educational Boarding & Day 16-22
No of pupils: B25 G25 No of boarders 50
Special Needs: DYS MLD PH PHe SpD SpL VIS
Non - maintained

RNIB RUSHTON HALL SCHOOL
Rushton, Kettering, Northamptonshire NN14 1RR
Tel: (0536) 710506
Head: D Hussey
Type: Co-educational Boarding & Day 5-12
No of pupils: B20 G10 No of boarders 28
Special Needs: Bl EBD MH MLD PH SLD SMH SpD VIS
Non - maintained

Nottinghamshire

PORTLAND COLLEGE
Nottingham Road, Mansfield,
Nottinghamshire NG18 4TJ
Tel: (0623) 792141
Head: P S Davis
Type: Co-educational Boarding & Day 16-59
No of pupils: 230 No of boarders 230
Special Needs: DYS MLD PH PHe SpD SpL VIS
Non - maintained

RUTLAND HOUSE SCHOOL
1 Elm Bank, Mapperley Road, Nottingham, NG3 5AJ
Tel: (0602) 621315
Head: Mrs C A Oviatt-Ham
Type: Co-educational Boarding & Day 4-17
No of pupils: B14 G11 No of boarders 18
Special Needs: Bl D EBD MH PH PHe SLD SMH SpD SpL VIS
Approved Independent

Oxfordshire

PENHURST SCHOOL
New Street, Chipping Norton,
Oxfordshire OX7 5LN
Tel: (0608) 642559
Head: D F Southeard
Type: Co-educational Boarding & Day 5-19
No of pupils: 30 No of boarders 30
Special Needs: PH PHe SLD SpD VIS
Non - maintained

Shropshire

CONDOVER HALL SCHOOL
Shrewsbury, Shropshire SY5 7AH
Tel: (0743) 722320
Head: A Jarvis
Type: Co-educational Boarding & Day 5-19
No of pupils: B58 G21 No of boarders 79
Special Needs: BI D EBD MH MLD PH PHe SpD SpL VIS
Non - maintained

DERWEN COLLEGE FOR THE DISABLED
Oswestry, Shropshire SY11 3JA
Tel: (0691) 661234
Head: D J Kendall
Type: Co-educational Boarding 16+ *No of pupils:* 164
Special Needs: D DYS EBD MH MLD PH PHe SLD SMH SpD SpL VIS
Approved Independent

Somerset

PRINCESS MARGARET SCHOOL
53 Middleway, Taunton, Somerset TA1 3QN
Tel: (0823) 257917
Head: D Walker
Type: Co-educational Boarding & Day 4-19
No of pupils: B38 G23 No of weekly boarders 43
Special Needs: MLD PH SpD SpL
Non - maintained

Staffordshire

BLADON HOUSE SCHOOL
Burton upon Trent, Newton Solney, Staffordshire DE15 0TA
Tel: (0283) 63787
Head: Mrs B W Brook
Type: Co-educational Boarding & Day 5-19
No of pupils: 60 No of boarders 56
Special Needs: D DYS MLD PH PHe SpD SpL
Approved Independent

LONGDON HALL
Longdon Green, Rugeley, Staffordshire WS15 4PT
Tel: (0543) 490634
Head: Mrs B W Brooks
Type: Co-educational 5-19
No of pupils: 50 No of weekly boarders 50
Special Needs: AUT
Approved Independent

PIPEWOOD SCHOOL
Blithbury Road, Blithbury, Rugeley, Staffordshire WS15 3JQ
Tel: (088922) 353
Head: A Otway
Type: Co-educational boarding
No of pupils: B44 G18 No of boarders 62
Approved Independent

Surrey

BANSTEAD PLACE ASSESSMENT & FURTHER EDUCATION CENTRE
Park Road, Banstead, Surrey SM7 3EE
Tel: (0737) 356222
Head: A R Gait
Type: Co-educational Boarding 16-30
No of pupils: B18 G17 No of boarders 35
Special Needs: EBD PH SpD SpL
Approved Independent

BURWOOD PARK SCHOOL AND COLLEGE
5 Eriswell Road, Walton-on-Thames,
Surrey KT12 5DQ
Tel: (0932) 227461
Head: M Kell
Type: Co-educational Boarding & Day 11-19
No of pupils: 65 No of boarders 65
Special Needs: D PHe
Non - maintained

THE GRANGE TRAINING CENTRE & SHELTERED WORKSHOP (for the Handicapped),
Rectory Lane, Bookham, Surrey KT23 4DZ
Tel: (0372) 452608
Head: Mrs C Gravestock
Type: Co-educational Boarding & Day 19-0
No of pupils: 50 No of boarders 50
Special Needs: D MLD PH PHe SpD
Non - maintained

MOOR HOUSE SCHOOL
Hurst Green, Oxted, Surrey RH8 9AQ
Tel: (0883) 712271
Head: J Lea
Type: Co-educational Boarding 7-16
No of pupils: B55 G25 No of boarders 80
Special Needs: SpD
Non - maintained

QUEEN ELIZABETH'S TRAINING COLLEGE
Leatherhead, Surrey KT22 0BN
Tel: (0372) 842204
Head: J S B Peake
Type: Co-educational Boarding & Day 18-60
No of pupils: 205 No of boarders 180
Special Needs: D EBD MLD PH PHe SpD VIS

RNIB HETHERSETT COLLEGE
Philanthropic Road, Redhill,
Surrey RH1 4DZ
Tel: (0737) 768935
Head: Dr M A Rowe
Type: Co-educational Boarding & Day 16-55
No of pupils: B60 G40 No of boarders 90
Special Needs: BI D EBD MLD PH PHe SpD SpL VIS
Non - maintained

Sensory or Physical Impairment

ROYAL SCHOOL FOR THE BLIND
Highlands Road, Leatherhead,
Surrey KT22 8NR
Tel: (0372) 373086
Head: R Perkins
Type: Co-educational Boarding & Day 19+
No of pupils: 140 No of boarders 140
Special Needs: BI VIS

ST DOMINICS SCHOOL
Hambledon, Godalming, Surrey GU8 4DX
Tel: (0428) 684693
Head: D Philipson
Type: Co-educational Boarding & Day 7-17
No of pupils: B78 G6 No of boarders 84
Special Needs: DYS PH PHe SpD SpL
Non - maintained

East Sussex

CHAILEY HERITAGE SCHOOL
North Chailey, East Sussex BN8 4EF
Tel: (082572) 2112
Head: H Parrott
Type: Co-educational Boarding & Day 2-19
Special Needs: MLD PH PHe SLD SpD SpL VIS
Non - maintained

HAMILTON LODGE SCHOOL
Walpole Road, Brighton,
East Sussex BN2 2ET
Tel: (0273) 682362
Head: Miss M M Moore
Type: Co-educational Boarding & Day 5-18
No of pupils: B31 G26 No of boarders 57
Special Needs: D
Approved Independent

OVINGDEAN HALL SCHOOL
Greenways, Brighton,
East Sussex BN2 7BJ
Tel: (0273) 301929
Head: D M Braybrook
Type: Co-educational Boarding & Day 11-16
No of pupils: B99 G69 No of boarders 168
Special Needs: D PHe
Non - maintained

PILGRIMS THE NATIONAL SCHOOL FOR ASTHMA & ECZEMA
Firle Road, Seaford, East Sussex BN25 2HX
Tel: (0323) 892697
Head: P B Murtagh
Type: Co-educational Boarding 9-19
No of pupils: B40 G35 No of boarders 75
Special Needs: DYS MLD
Non - maintained

ST MARY'S SCHOOL
Wrestwood Road, Bexhill-on-Sea, East Sussex TN40 2LU
Tel: (0424) 730740
Head: D Cassar
Type: Co-educational Boarding & Day 5-16
No of pupils: B41 G36 No of boarders 69
Special Needs: DYS EBD MLD PH PHe SpD SpL VIS
Approved Independent

West Sussex

INGLEFIELD MANOR SCHOOL
Five Oaks, Billingshurst, West Sussex RH14 9AX
Tel: (0403) 782294
Head: Mrs C Donovan
Type: Co-educational Boarding & Day 3-11
No of pupils: 50 No of boarders 32
Special Needs: CP PH
Approved Independent

MILL HALL ORAL SCHOOL FOR THE DEAF
Whiteman's Green, Cuckfield, West Sussex RH17 5HX
Tel: (0444) 454000
Head: M Brown
Type: Co-educational Boarding & Day 4-12
No of pupils: B28 G27 No of weekly boarders 42
Special Needs: D PHe
Approved Independent

RNIB SUNSHINE HOUSE SCHOOL
Dunnings Road, East Grinstead, West Sussex RH19 4ND
Tel: (0342) 323141
Head: M P Shaw
Type: Co-educational Boarding & Day 2-8
No of pupils: B6 G2 No of boarders 8
Special Needs: BI D EBD MH MLD PH PHe SLD SMH SpD VIS
Non - maintained

Tyne and Wear

NORTHERN COUNTIES SCHOOL FOR THE DEAF
Great North Road, Newcastle-Upon-Tyne,
Tyne and Wear NE2 3BB
Tel: 091 281 5821
Head: K J C Lewis
Type: Co-educational Boarding & Day 3-21
No of pupils: B61 G32 No of boarders 45
Special Needs: BI D PHe SpD VIS
Non - maintained

PERCY HEDLEY SCHOOL
Forest Hall, Tyne and Wear NE12 8YY
Tel: (091) 266 5451
Head: J Ferris
Type: Co-educational Boarding & Day 3-16
No of pupils: B90 G50 No of boarders 30
Special Needs: CP MLD PH SpD SpL
Non - maintained

West Midlands

HEREWARD COLLEGE OF FURTHER EDUCATION
Bramston Crescent, Tile Hill Lane, Coventry,
West Midlands CV4 9SW
Tel: (0203) 461231
Head: W R Williams
Type: Co-educational Boarding & Day 16+
No of pupils: B60 G60 No of boarders 120
Special Needs: PH PHe SLD SpD VIS

QUEEN ALEXANDRA COLLEGE
49 Court Oak Road, Harborne, Birmingham,
West Midlands B17 9TG
Tel: (021) 427 4577
Head: T S Gould
Type: Co-educational Boarding & Day 16-55
No of pupils: B100 G50 No of boarders 130
Special Needs: Bl D MLD PH PHe SLD SpL VIS
Approved Independent

North Yorkshire

HENSHAW'S COLLEGE
Bogs Lane, Harrogate, North Yorkshire HG1 4ED
Tel: (0423) 886451
Head: S C Jones
Type: Co-educational Boarding & Day 14-19
No of pupils: B50 G50 No of boarders 70
Special Needs: Bl D MLD PH PHe SLD SpD VIS
Approved Independent

South Yorkshire

DONCASTER COLLEGE FOR THE DEAF
Leger Way, Doncaster, South Yorkshire DN2 6AY
Tel: (0302) 342166
Head: R Brown Dickson
Type: Co-educational Boarding & Day 4-16
No of pupils: B59 G31 No of boarders 35
Special Needs: D PHe
Non - maintained

West Yorkshire

HAWKSWORTH HALL SCHOOL
Guiseley, Leeds, West Yorkshire LS20 8NU
Tel: (0943) 870058
Head: M Worrall
Type: Co-educational Boarding & Day 0-12
No of pupils: B15 G15 No of boarders 18
Special Needs: Bl D PH PHe SLD SpD VIS
Non - maintained

HOLLY BANK SCHOOL
Roe Head, Far Common Road, Mirfield,
West Yorkshire WF14 0DQ
Tel: (0924) 490833
Head: T S Hodkinson
Type: Co-educational Boarding & Day 5-19
No of pupils: B22 G10 No of boarders 29
Special Needs: MLD PH PHe SLD SpD VIS
Non - maintained

ST JOHN'S R C SCHOOL
Church Street, Boston Spa, Wetherby, West Yorkshire LS23 6DF
Tel: (0937) 842144
Head: Sister C Mathews
Type: Co-educational Boarding & Day 3-18
No of pupils: B62 G52 No of boarders 84
Special Needs: D PHe
Non - maintained

SCOTLAND

Aberdeenshire

THE CAMPHILL RUDOLF STEINER SCHOOLS
Central Office, Murtle Estate, Bieldside, Aberdeenshire AB1 9EP
Tel: (0224) 867935
Type: Co-educational Boarding & Day 5-19
No of pupils: B114 G40 No of boarders 160
Special Needs: BI D DYS EBD MH MLD PH PHe SLD SMH SpD SpL VIS
Independent

Lanarkshire

ALEXANDER ANDERSON HOME
Thornlea Park, Wishaw, Lanarkshire
Tel: (0698) 372003
Head: D Canern
Type: Co-educational Day 5-16

STANMORE HOUSE RESIDENTIAL SCHOOL
Lanark, Lanarkshire ML11 7RR
Tel: (0555) 65041
Head: Mrs J Bridges
Type: Co-educational Boarding & Day 2-19
No of pupils: B48 G31 No of boarders 51
Special Needs: PH SLD SMH SpD

Midlothian

DONALDSON'S SCHOOL FOR THE DEAF
West Coates, Edinburgh, Midlothian EH12 5JJ
Tel: (031) 9911
Head: J Miller
Type: Co-educational Boarding & Day 3-19
No of pupils: B47 G25 No of boarders 24
Special Needs: D PHe SpD
Approved Independent

ROYAL BLIND SCHOOL
Craigmillar Park, Edinburgh, Midlothian EH16 5NA
Tel: (031) 667 1100
Head: Mrs M L S Meek
Type: Co-educational Boarding & Day 3-19
No of pupils: B62 G31 No of boarders 75
Special Needs: BI MLD PH PHe SLD VIS

WESTERLEA SCHOOL
11 Ellersly Road, Edinburgh, Midlothian EH12 6HY
Tel: (031) 337 1236
Head: Mrs M Thompson
Type: Co-educational Day 3-18
Special Needs: CP PH
Approved Independent

Renfrewshire

CORSEFORD SCHOOL
Milliken Park, Kilbarchan, Renfrewshire PA10 2NT
Tel: (05057) 2141/3
Head: Mrs M Boyle
Type: Co-educational Boarding & Day to 19
No of pupils: B27 G23 No of boarders 30
Special Needs: PH SpL

WALES

South Glamorgan

CRAIG-Y-PARC SCHOOL
Pentyrch, Cardiff, South Glamorgan CF4 8NB
Tel: (0222) 890397
Head: Mrs M Fowler
Type: Co-educational Boarding & Day 4-16
No of pupils: 49
Special Needs: MLD PH PHe SpD
Non - maintained

NORTHERN IRELAND

County Antrim

JORDANSTOWN SCHOOLS
85 Jordanstown Road, Newtownabbey, County Antrim BT37 0QE
Tel: (0232) 863541
Head: J G McClelland
Type: Co-educational Boarding & Day 4-19
No of pupils: B59 G59 No of boarders 31
Special Needs: BI D PHe VIS

NATIONAL ASSOCIATION OF INDEPENDENT AND NON-MAINTAINED SPECIAL SCHOOLS

(NAIMS)

The National Association of Independent and Non-Maintained Special Schools (NAIMS) was established in 1985 by a group of Headteachers who believed there was a real need for the expertise developed over many years to be shared.

The Association has grown since those early days and can now be said to represent the independent and non-maintained sector in special education.

Recently NAIMS has published a Code of Good Practice which will help to ensure that children with special needs will continue to receive the best in education - particularly residential - and care. The Association recognises the importance of working in partnership with families and professionals.

NAIMS has appointed a Professional Development Officer who is involved in the ongoing development of staff training within the Association.

Conferences are organised and a Newsletter produced, ensuring that member schools are kept up to date on training issues.

For further information about NAIMS contact the Membership Secretary: F.H. Green, Esq, 6 Nelson Street, Deal, Kent CT14 6DD.

Display Listings of Schools and Colleges specialising in Sensory & Physical Impairment

Sensory & Physical Impairment

Bethesda School

(Founded 1890)

*57A Schools Hill,
Cheadle,
Cheshire SK8 1JE*
Tel: 061 428 7897 Fax: 061 491 5056

Head: Carl Evans, DipEd
Age range: 11-19. Boarders from 11-19
No. of pupils enrolled as at 1.9.91: 50
27 Boys   23 Girls
Fees per annum: Day: £12,780; Boarding: £19,170

Type: Day/Boarding School for physical disabilities, associated learning difficulties, Autistic Unit

Member of: NAIMS

Curriculum: A planned programme of individual assessment and monitoring, leading to programmes of study implemented by a multi-disciplinary team. Small groups (ratio 1:3) specialising in language and communication teaching, but with access to National Curriculum.

Entry requirements: Pupils who would benefit from intensive, individual programmes, who need speech, occupational or physio-therapy. 24 hour medical cover, especially those with multiple disabilities or autistic behaviours.

PROSPECTUSES
MINI-PROSPECTUSES
NEWSLETTERS
EXHIBITION MATERIALS
MARKETING
VIDEO FILMS
SCHOOL MAGAZINES
SCHOOL YEAR BOOKS

John Catt Educational Limited

Great Glemham
Saxmundham
Suffolk IP17 2DH

Tel: 0728 78 666
Fax: 0728 78 415

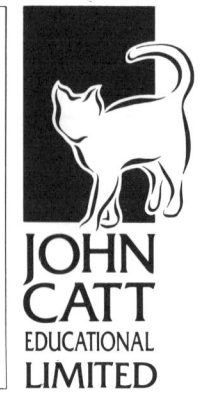

JOHN CATT EDUCATIONAL LIMITED

Birkdale School for Hearing Impaired Children

(Founded 1948)

*40 Lancaster Road,
Birkdale, Southport,
Merseyside PR8 2JY*
Tel: 0704 67220

Principal: Mr Edward Loxham, BEd, MEd (Aud.)
Age range: 4-19. Boarders from 4
No. of pupils enrolled as at 1.9.91: 147
Infant/Junior: 24 Boys 31 Girls; Senior: 47 Boys 35 Girls;
Further Education: 4 Boys 6 Girls
Fees per annum: Infant: Day £8694, Boarding £11,484
Day: £9286, Boarding: £12,900
Further Education: Day £6501, Boarding £8991

Type: Co-educational School for children with severe and profound hearing impairment

Religious denomination: Non-denominational

Member of: NPRA (Accredited Centre for Northern Partnership for Records of Achievement)

Curriculum: Traditional core subjects as well as Art, Craft and Design Technology, Communications, Home Economics, Textiles and Dance and Drama, reflecting the requirements of the National Curriculum. Individual tuition given as needed in order to help to develop spoken language. Group teaching of up to eight pupils. Wide choice of further education at 16+ in partnership with local colleges of further education.

Entry requirements: Non-selective. Available to all children best able to benefit from an auditory/oral education.

Examinations offered: 10 subjects at GCSE (NEA) (ULEAC) (MEG). RSA Computer Studies, ROAs (Records of Achievement), NPRA (Northern Partnership for Records of Achievement.

Academic and leisure facilities: Accoustically

treated rooms with powerful group amplification systems, modern audiology department, computer room, CDT workshop, science laboratory, art studio. 12 acres of playing fields with football, cricket and hockey pitches, and full size athletics track. Tennis and badminton courts. A fully equipped gymnasium and a heated indoor swimming pool.

Craig-y-Parc School

(Founded 1955)

Heol-y-Parc, Pentyrch, Nr Cardiff CF4 8NB
Tel: 0222 890397 Fax: 0222 891404

Head: Mrs M. Fowler, BEd, DipSpecEd, DEM
Age range: 4+-16. Boarders from 7+
No. of pupils enrolled as at 1.1.92: 49
Junior: 15 Boys 11 Girls; Senior: 19 Boys 4 Girls
Fees per annum: Day: £13,689
Weekly Boarding: £20,535; Full Boarding: £22,818

Type: An independent residential special school catering for pupils with Cerebral Palsy and associated communication and sensory disabilities.

Member of: The Spastics Society

Curriculum: Modified and giving access to National Curriculum.

Entry requirements: A Statement of Special Educational Needs and/or a Spastics Society assessment with recommendation, together with confirmation of financial sponsorship.

We specialise in consultancy, design, production and publication of:

- [✓] Prospectuses
- [✓] Mini-prospectuses
- [✓] Newsletters
- [✓] Exhibition Materials
- [✓] Marketing
- [✓] Video Films
- [✓] School Magazines
- [✓] School Year Books

Our experience and quality of craftsmanship enable us to give a service which we believe is unequalled by any other organisation at a highly competitive price.

John Catt Educational Limited
Great Glemham,
Saxmundham,
Suffolk IP17 2DH
Tel: 0728 78 666   Fax: 0728 78 415

Don't forget to make use of the Reader Enquiry Service cards at the back of the Guide if you want more information about the Schools or Colleges listed.

Normal curriculum schools with facilities to help pupils with Dyslexia or Special Learning Needs appear in Section Four.

Chailey Heritage School

(Founded 1903)

*North Chailey,
Lewes,
East Sussex BN8 4EF
Tel: 082 572 2112 Fax: 082 572 3544*

Head: Mr Hugh Parrott, CertEd, Dip Spec Ed
(Member of NAHT, NAIMS)
Age range: 2½-19. Boarders from 7 (with exceptions)
No. of pupils enrolled as at 1.9.91: 103
Pre-School: 4 Boys 4 Girls; Junior: 15 Boys 12 Girls
Senior: 24 Boys 29 Girls; Upper School: 8 Boys 7 Girls
Fees per annum: Not made available to parents

Type: Non-Maintained Physical, Multiple and Complex Disabilities

Entry requirements: Informal visits welcomed. Referrals must come from Education Authorities. Formal visit followed by joint discipline meeting to ascertain benefits of placement. Agreement re: funding by pupils' Heath Authority must be reached - application made by Chailey Heritage.

Chailey Heritage has a Charter of Rights of Children which explicitly states that each child has these fundamental rights:-

to be valued as an individual

to be treated with dignity and respect

to be loved and cared for as a child first

to be safe

Curriculum: The curriculum is defined as all learning opportunities. It enables children to achieve choice and control of their environment by developing:-

English, Mathematics, Social & Emotional Skills, Posture Management, Fine & Gross Motor Skills, Self Care.

Teachers are fully conversant with the philosophy and details of the National Curriculum. Wherever Attainments Targets, Programmes of Study and Standard Assessment Tasks are seen to be beneficial to pupils, they are reflected in the work of that child and group.

Pre-School: Provides an interdisciplinary assessment for children with Special Needs.

Fosters growth and development.

Provides structured activities to promote the acquisition of skills in areas of language and communication; gross and fine motor development; cognition and play; social and emotional development; sensory awareness; self help.

Monitors physical and medical need.

Assists in advice over the provision of assistive devices for posture, mobility and self-care.

Junior School: Development of basic skills - language, communication, posture, mobility and physical skills.

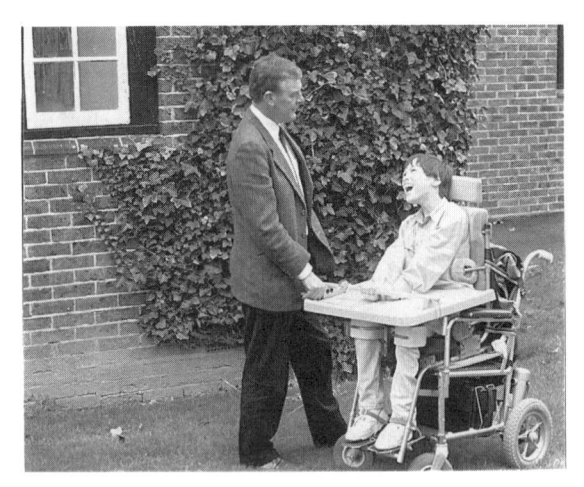

Senior School: Development of basic skills; functional language and physical development; City & Guilds Foundation Programme, TVEX. Social and living skills.

Upper School: Emphasis placed on provision of courses that concentrate on the development of students' independence and preparation for transition from school to adult life.

Academic and leisure facilities: Riding Centre, Swimming/Therapy Pool, Educational and Leisure outings, in school and community based youth clubs, Scouts, Cubs, Guides, Brownies. Holiday Play Schemes.

Close association with Brighton Health Authority.

Consultants, Therapists, Nurses, Engineers.

Chailey Heritage based technicians. Health Visitor. Social Services. Voluntary Services Manager.

Dorton House School

Royal London Society for the Blind

(Founded 1838)

*Seal,
Nr Sevenoaks,
Kent TN15 0ED
Tel: 0732 61477 Fax: 0732 63363*

Head: Dr Jean Chadha
Age range: 4-16. Boarders from 5 exceptionally
No. of pupils enrolled as at 1.1.92: 114
Junior: 33 Boys 28 Girls; Senior: 29 Boys 24 Girls
There is a College of FE (Dorton College) on-site for 16+ students
Fees per annum: Day: £12,225
Boarding: £16,299

Type: Blind and partially sighted

Religious denomination: None

Member of: Non-maintained Schools and Colleges for the Visually Handicapped

Curriculum: The School follows the full National Curriculum with additions for the handicap. These include mobility and orientation skills, braille, handwriting, information technology for the visually impaired, health education, living skills. Students are prepared for GCSE courses from a wide range of 15 subjects.

Entry requirements: All pupils who have a severe visual impairment are eligible for entry and are referred to us for assessment by parents or LEAs.

Examinations offered: GCSE examinations using SEG, MEG, ULEAG, NEAB, RSA, Pitmans.

Dorton House is uniquely well equipped for the education of blind and partially sighted students. It has a particularly well equipped Science, Home Economics and Art and CDT rooms in both the Primary and Secondary Departments. Classrooms are fully equipped with specialist devices for blind and partially sighted pupils, including computers, electronic Braillers and CCTVs.

There is a splendid Assembly Hall, a Gymnasium, an indoor swimming pool, a fitness centre, an outdoor activities obstacle course, all-weather football pitch and all weather surfaces for cricket and athletics.

All forms of outdoor activities, including climbing, canoeing, sailing, caving, camping, hiking are followed and the School has an activities centre in the Brecon Beacons. All students are encouraged to fully participate in these activities.

PROSPECTUSES
MINI-PROSPECTUSES
NEWSLETTERS
EXHIBITION MATERIALS
MARKETING
VIDEO FILMS
SCHOOL MAGAZINES
SCHOOL YEAR BOOKS

John Catt Educational Limited

Great Glemham
Saxmundham
Suffolk IP17 2DH

Tel 0728 78 666
Fax 0728 78 415

JOHN CATT EDUCATIONAL LIMITED

Authoritative articles covering many important aspects of Special Learning Needs appear at the start of the Guide. Parents are urged to read them.

Halliwick College

(Founded)

*Bush Hill Road,
Winchmore Hill, London N21 2DU
Tel: 081 360 2442*

Based in North London, we offer a wide range of residential and day courses in Further Education for students of 16+ with all types of disability.

Provision includes:

Specialised packages to support student access to mainstream courses.

Various examination courses including City & Guilds, CPVE ESB.

Intensive independence and life-skills training on site and in community units, supervised by specialist tutors, therapists and facilitators.

Day courses for students with additional sensory impairment.

We have a positive attitude towards integration and equal opportunities both educationally and within the community and are developing close links with Enfield College.

It is envisaged that during 1993 we will be re-sited within the campus of Enfield College opening up much closer access to the curriculum on offer there, while continuing to supply specialised courses and support services within a new resource centre by experienced and well qualified staff.

The curriculum offers highly specialised remedial, general education and vocational opportunities to encourage learning potentials for all students.

A continuous profiling system is in operation to give supportive feedback to students and maintain quality control.

For information please contact Julie Durham, College Manager.

Hawksworth Hall School

(Founded 1958)

*Hawksworth,
Guiseley,
Leeds LS20 8NU
Tel: 0943 870058 Fax: 0943 870038*

Head: Martyn W. Worrall, MA
Age range: 4-12. Boarders from 4
No. of pupils enrolled as at 1.1.92: 20
8 Boys 12 Girls
Fees per annum: Day: £18,916
Weekly Boarding: £28,366, Termly Boarding £31,519

Type: Profound and Severe Learning and Physical Difficulties

Member of: The Spastics Society for people with Cerebral Palsy

Curriculum: All children who attend Hawksworth Hall have full access to the National Curriculum. There are three teaching groups in the main school with six/seven children in each. Teams of therapists, care staff and volunteers support each class. Children follow individually designed programmes throughout our extended educational day.

Entry requirements: Children's individual special educational needs are identified by separate 1981 Act and School-based assessments. Children may be sponsored by LEAs or be supported by private funding.

Academic and leisure facilities: Our extended educational day enables us to provide individual feeding, dressing, communication and exercise programmes which complement in-class work. We have extensive, very attractive grounds and all children have access to a wide range of appropriate recreational activities. The School is very much part of the local community.

Ingfield Manor School

(Founded 1961)

*Five Oaks,
Billinghurst,
West Sussex RH14 9AX*
Tel: 0403 782294/784241 Fax: 0403 785066

Head: Mrs Cherryl Donovan, DipEd
Age range: 0-5 (School for Parents)
3-11 (Main School)
No. of pupils enrolled as at 1.1.92:
School for Parents: 35; Main School: 40
(Main School is in process of expanding to take 50 pupils)
Fees per annum:
Day: To be advised; Weekly Boarding: To be advised;
There are no fees for School for Parents

Type: Day and Weekly Boarding for children with Cerebral Palsy of average or above average intelligence. Children with severe behavioural/emotional problems or continuous poor health are not usually accepted. Catchment area is national.

The School is run by The Spastics Society

Children are given full access to mainstream National Curriculum core and foundation subjects. The curriculum is based on a holistic view of children and their intellectual, emotional and social needs. Technology features strongly and is used to support the children as they extend their repertoire of skills.

The School is working towards Conductive Education and specialises in providing programmes advised and supported by the Peto Institute in Budapest. Staff work in inter-disciplinary teams and are responsible for the needs of the children throughout the day.

Medical oversight is provided by orthopaedic, neuropaediatric and paediatric consultants as well as a full range of visiting specialists. Two nurses are on staff, available 24 hours a day.

The children have access to the immediate school environment including the swimming pool (on site), horse riding (local RDA) and organized outings to places of interest. Social and leisure periods are regarded as important extensions to the curriculum.

Don't forget to make use of the Reader Enquiry Service cards at the back of the Guide if you want more information about the Schools or Colleges listed.

We specialise in consultancy, design, production and publication of:

- ☑ **Prospectuses**
- ☑ **Mini-prospectuses**
- ☑ **Newsletters**
- ☑ **Exhibition Materials**
- ☑ **Marketing**
- ☑ **Video Films**
- ☑ **School Magazines**
- ☑ **School Year Books**

Our experience and quality of craftsmanship enable us to give a service which we believe is unequalled by any other organisation at a highly competitive price.

John Catt Educational Limited
Great Glemham,
Saxmundham,
Suffolk IP17 2DH
Tel: 0728 78 666 Fax: 0728 78 415

LORD MAYOR TRELOAR COLLEGE
ALTON, HAMPSHIRE.

(Founded 1908)

**Upper School,
Holybourne, Alton,
Hampshire GU34 4EN
Tel: 0420 83508 Fax: 0420 23957**

Headmaster: Hartley Heard, MA, MCollP
(Member of SHA, SHMIS)
Age range: 8-19. Boarders from 8-19
No. of pupils enrolled as at 1.1.92: 277
Junior: 14 Boys 7 Girls; Senior: 64 Boys 42 Girls
Sixth Form: 95 Boys 53 Girls
Fees per annum: Day: £17,682
Boarding: £23,577

Type: Non-maintained, residential, co-educational. All Physical Disabilities and associated Learning Difficulties

Religious denomination: Non-denominational

Member of: NAIMS, NATSPEC, BSA

Curriculum: National Curriculum for all up to 16; A level: CPVE; CGLI; students with Learning Difficulties follow curricula suited to their individual needs; Lifeskills courses.

Entry requirements: Future students must attend for a day's assessment by different staff in academic, medical, therapy and rehabilitation engineering. Each student must be able to benefit from placement.

Examinations offered: GCSE, (MEG, NEA, SEG); B.Tec; City and Guilds; CPVE; Pitmans; Royal Society of Arts; AEB Basic Skills; A level (taken usually at Alton College).

Academic and leisure facilities: New facilities for Technology, Art, Design, Photography. Music recording studio. Computer rooms. Two libraries. Two indoor heated pools; hydrotherapy pool. Sports include basketball, swimming, athletics, archery, shooting.

Meldreth Manor School

*Fenny Lane,
Meldreth, Royston,
Herts SG8 6LG
Tel: 0763 260771 Fax: 0763 263361*

Acting Head Teacher: Caroline Coles
Age range: 8-19
No. of pupils enrolled as at 1.1.92: 77
Fees per annum: Day: £18,278
Weekly Boarding: £26,440; Full Boarding: £29,156

Type: Physical disabilities with severe learning difficulties. Specialising in additional sensory impairment.

Curriculum: Every pupil follows an individual learning programme within a core of subjects. The school curriculum documents reflect recent changes in legislation and have taken full account of the National Curriculum.

The specific content of each pupil's learning package is determined through a process of regular reviews and assessment, involving all of the staff who work with the pupil and following detailed consultation with parents. The School has a detailed recording system and is accredited by the Cambridge Partnership for Record of Achievements.

Pupils are provided with a seven day learning programme and teams of staff consisting of teachers, student support workers, nurses, physiotherapists and speech therapists, ensure a consistency of approach and management for all pupils.

Entry requirements: For informal visit, assessment for placement, please contact Head Teacher.

A full range of guides to UK Schools is also published by John Catt Educational.

We specialise in consultancy, design, production and publication of:

- ☑ **Prospectuses**
- ☑ **Mini-prospectuses**
- ☑ **Newsletters**
- ☑ **Exhibition Materials**
- ☑ **Marketing**
- ☑ **Video Films**
- ☑ **School Magazines**
- ☑ **School Year Books**

Our experience and quality of craftsmanship enable us to give a service which we believe is unequalled by any other organisation at a highly competitive price.

For more details please telephone or write to:

John Catt Educational Limited
Great Glemham,
Saxmundham,
Suffolk IP17 2DH

Tel: 0728 78 666   Fax: 0728 78 415

Ovingdean Hall School

(Founded 1841)

*Greenways,
Brighton,
East Sussex BN2 7BJ
Tel: 0273 301929 Fax: 0273 305884*

Head: David M. Braybrook, MA, FRSA
Age range: 11-16+. Weekly Boarders from 11
No. of pupils enrolled as at 1.1.92: 169
Senior: 89 Boys 62 Girls; FE (16+): 11 Boys 7 Girls
Fees per term: Day: £3688
Weekly Boarding/FE: £4843; Full Boarding: £6104

Type: Non-maintained Special School offering weekly boarding and day education to secondary aged/Further Education pupils/students who are hearing impaired

Religious denomination: Non-denominational

Member of: Association of Non-Maintained Special Schools

Curriculum: A broad and balanced curriculum with a high level of support is available to all pupils throughout the school in order to give them the widest possible opportunity of the development in academic, technical, practical and creative areas. The emphasis throughout the school's programme is on the individual child. Extensive pastoral and tutorial systems exist to ensure individual needs are identified and met including access to an Audiologist, a Counsellor, Speech Therapist and Educational Psychologist. The work of the school is directed towards the delivery of the National Curriculum, while retaining particular elements and emphasis which recognise the special educational needs arising from hearing impairment. The school is committed to a natural aural philosophy which aims to develop spoken language as a means of communication. Sign language is not used.

Entry requirements: Parents may visit the School on an informal basis. The School is non-selective and pupils are funded by their Local Education Authority. Part of the admission procedure is to formally interview the child in order to assess his/her needs and to determine how these needs might best be met.

Examinations offered: 14-16 Foundation Programme; GCSE and Mature Syllabus; CPVE.

Academic and leisure facilities: Specialist Classrooms, Audiology Centre, Library, Art and Design Block, Gymnasium, Swimming Pool, Technology Block, Music and Drama Rooms.

A full range of guides to UK Schools is also published by John Catt Educational.

We specialise in consultancy, design, production and publication of:

- ☑ **Prospectuses**
- ☑ **Mini-prospectuses**
- ☑ **Newsletters**
- ☑ **Exhibition Materials**
- ☑ **Marketing**
- ☑ **Video Films**
- ☑ **School Magazines**
- ☑ **School Year Books**

Our experience and quality of craftsmanship enable us to give a service which we believe is unequalled by any other organisation at a highly competitive price.

John Catt Educational Limited
Great Glemham,
Saxmundham,
Suffolk IP17 2DH
Tel: 0728 78 666 Fax: 0728 78 415

Penhurst School

(Founded 1923)

*New Street,
Chipping Norton,
Oxfordshire OX7 5LN
Tel: 0608 642559*

ND

Head: Mr David Southeard, BSc (Hons), BPhil (Ed)
Age range: 5-19. Boarders from 5
No. of pupils enrolled as at 1.1.92: 32
Junior: 8 Boys 5 Girls; Senior: 12 Boys 7 Girls
Fees per annum: On application

Type: Residential School for children with physical disabilities and learning difficulties. Administered by the National Children's Home

Religious denomination: Methodist

Member of: NAHT, NASEN, NAIMS

Curriculum: We make provision for children to study the subjects of the National Curriculum at a level appropriate to their level of development. At present this equates to Levels 1-3, though some children will be working within Level 1 for many years. All children follow a carefully structured curriculum that emphasises and records progress and achievement.

The National Curriculum is supplemented by other subjects *eg* Personal and Social Education as appropriate.

Entry requirements: Children between the age of 5 and 19 years with physical disabilities and severe/profound learning difficulties whose home lies within two hours travelling time from the School.

We specialise in consultancy, design, production and publication of:

- [✓] **Prospectuses**
- [✓] **Mini-prospectuses**
- [✓] **Newsletters**
- [✓] **Exhibition Materials**
- [✓] **Marketing**
- [✓] **Video Films**
- [✓] **School Magazines**
- [✓] **School Year Books**

Our experience and quality of craftsmanship enable us to give a service which we believe is unequalled by any other organisation at a highly competitive price.

John Catt Educational Limited
Great Glemham,
Saxmundham,
Suffolk IP17 2DH
Tel: 0728 78 666   Fax: 0728 78 415

Normal curriculum schools with facilities to help pupils with Dyslexia or Special Learning Needs appear in Section Four.

RNIB Condover Hall School

(Founded 1948)

*Condover,
Nr Shrewsbury,
Shropshire SY5 7AH
Tel: 0743 722320*

Head: Mr A Jarvis
Age range: 11-19 (deaf-blind: 4-19). Boarders from 11-19 (deaf-blind: 4-19)
No. of pupils enrolled as at 1.1.92: 78
Senior boys: 56 Senior girls: 22
Range of fees per annum (incl VAT) as at 1.1.92 (payable by LEA):
Day: from £16,968
Boarding: from £25,452

Type: Non-maintained special school for visually handicapped pupils with additional handicaps; also, deaf-blind pupils.

Religious affiliation: None

Maintained by: Royal National Institute for the Blind

Curriculum: The School provides a wide range of learning experiences, and children are encouraged to use any sight they may have, as well as other sensory channels. The curriculum emphasises self-awareness, making relationships with others and the development of independence and mobility skills. Trained child care staff deliver a scheme of self-care and social skills development. Children have access to the National Curriculum. The Pathways Unit meets the needs of deaf-blind children.

Entry requirements: Boys and girls with significant degrees of visual handicap, together with one or more additional handicaps. The Pathways Unit takes deaf-blind pupils aged 4-19 years and provides a programme of communication development, including oral and signed speech, finger spelling, print or braille reading and writing.

Leavers' adviser: A senior teacher has full-time responsibility for liaison with families and local authority services to assist pupils preparing to leave the School.

Academic and leisure facilities: The campus includes extensive teaching, administrative and training accommodation, together with family flats and an indoor pool. Children enjoy many leisure activities, with trips and longer visits. Parents' weekends are arranged, and visits from parents are encouraged at any time, with accommodation available for this purpose.

Royal National Institute for the Blind

PROSPECTUSES
MINI-PROSPECTUSES
NEWSLETTERS
EXHIBITION MATERIALS
MARKETING
VIDEO FILMS
SCHOOL MAGAZINES
SCHOOL YEAR BOOKS

John Catt Educational Limited

Great Glemham
Saxmundham
Suffolk IP17 2DH

Tel: 0728 78 666
Fax: 0728 78 415

JOHN CATT EDUCATIONAL LIMITED

RNIB Hethersett College

(Founded 1956)

Philanthropic Road, Redhill, Surrey RH1 4DZ
Tel: 0737 768935 Fax: 0737 765907

Head: Dr M. Rowe, PhD, MSc, DLC, MIBiol
Age range: 16+. Boarders from 16+
No. of pupils enrolled as at 1.1.92: 98
Fees per annum: Day: £13,365 -£14,412
Boarding: £21,000 - £24,000

Type: College of Further Education and Vocational Training for the visually impaired

Member of: NATSPEC (National Association of Specialist Colleges)

Curriculum: The College offers four types of course: Life Skills; Foundation Course; Pre-Vocational Education (CPVE); Vocational Training Courses.

Entry requirements: All students are visually impaired. Many have additional disabilities/needs. Entry according to individual assessment and interview.

RNIB
Royal National Institute for the Blind

PROSPECTUSES
MINI-PROSPECTUSES
NEWSLETTERS
EXHIBITION MATERIALS
MARKETING
VIDEO FILMS
SCHOOL MAGAZINES
SCHOOL YEAR BOOKS

John Catt Educational Limited
Great Glemham
Saxmundham
Suffolk IP17 2DH
Tel 0728 78 666
Fax 0728 78 415

JOHN CATT EDUCATIONAL LIMITED

RNIB New College

(Founded 1866)

Whittington Road, Worcester WR5 2JX
Tel: 0905 763933
Fax: 0905 763277

Head: Rev B.R. Manthorp, MA
Age range: 9-19. Boarders from 9-19
No. of pupils enrolled as at 1.1.92: 121
Junior: 5 Boys 2 Girls; Senior: 52 Boys 32 Girls
Sixth Form: 24 Boys 7 Girls
Fees payable by LEA in which the pupil resides

Type: A co-educational residential school for pupils with a severe visual impairment who are able to follow an academic curriculum

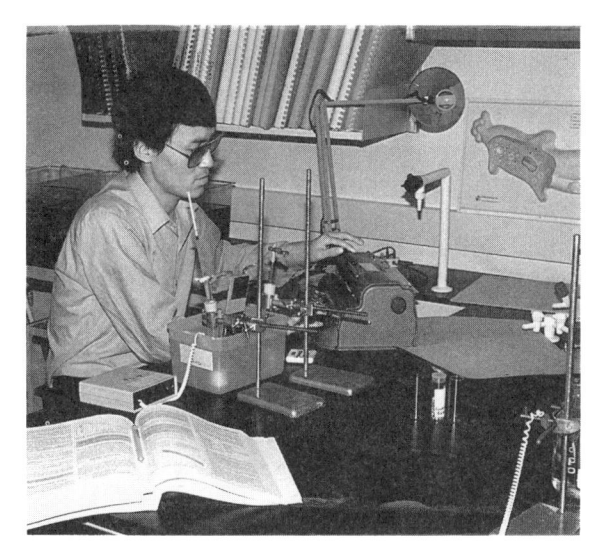

Religious denomination: Church of England/All denominations accepted

Member of: HMC, ISIS

Curriculum: Our curriculum is geared towards those with a visual impairment (however severe) who are able to follow a broadly based academic curriculum up to GCSEs and then A levels. In addition we cover those subjects which are particularly appropriate to those with impaired vision - daily living skills, keyboard skills, mobility.

Entry requirements: Our main entry time is in September of each year but prospective pupils may be assessed at any age or time appropriate to them. An application form for assessment may be obtained from the school. All prospective parents and pupils are encouraged to visit the school first.

Examinations offered: 18 GCSE, MEG & SEG. 18 A level. Oxford & Cambridge, Oxford, Cambridge, ULEAC, JMB.

Academic and leisure facilities: Pupils have the wide range of specialist rooms available to them necessary for the academic curriculum. Leisure activities abound in the form of after school clubs and good use is made of both the schools' facilities and those round about.

Pupils gradually acquire the daily living skills needed for them to live an independent fulfilled student and adult life, as they move from a first year house to a middle school house and then to a sixth form hostel.

The School aims to fit the pupils academically and practically for adult life, so that they can take their place in society on equal terms with their sighted peers. This is no mean feat when you consider that all are visually impaired, many with a severe impairment, and some have an additional handicap.

In order to achieve this we must be sure that they reach their academic potential, and, they have the necessary skills in order that they can look after themselves. To this end the pupils have lessons in daily living skills, and these skills are put into practice in the residential situation, first of all under the guidance of house mothers, and later on a more independent basis in the sixth form block. This hostel is akin to a university or polytechnic hostel. Students are expected to look after all their meals, except the mid-day meal during the week, their own laundry, in the laundry room in their block, the planning of their work, their leisure, and their contribution to the community, as well as sorting out their own future and all that that entails: reading prospecti, filling in forms, travelling to and attending interviews. No mean feat for their sighted contemporaries, our pupils must achieve the same standards.

In the past our pupils have gone on to careers in physiotherapy, teaching, law, music, the church, all fairly predictable for visually impaired people. Recent technology has opened up numerous new careers, previously thought unsuitable, computing, farming, business management, and perhaps the most unlikely - designing helicopter engines!

Royal National Institute for the Blind

A full range of guides to UK Schools is also published by John Catt Educational.

We specialise in consultancy, design, production and publication of:

- [✓] **Prospectuses**
- [✓] **Mini-prospectuses**
- [✓] **Newsletters**
- [✓] **Exhibition Materials**
- [✓] **Marketing**
- [✓] **Video Films**
- [✓] **School Magazines**
- [✓] **School Year Books**

Our experience and quality of craftsmanship enable us to give a service which we believe is unequalled by any other organisation at a highly competitive price.

John Catt Educational Limited
Great Glemham,
Saxmundham,
Suffolk IP17 2DH
Tel: 0728 78 666   Fax: 0728 78 415

RNIB Rushton Hall School

(Founded 1960)

*Rushton,
Nr Kettering,
Northants NN14 1RR
Tel: 0536 710506 Fax: 0536 418506*

Head: Mr D Hussey
Age range: 8-12. Boarders from 8-12
No. of pupils enrolled as at 1.1.92: 30
Boys: 20 Girls: 10
Range of fees per annum (incl VAT) as at 1.1.92
(payable by LEA): Day: from £18,006
Boarding: from £27,006

Type: Non-maintained special School for visually handicapped pupils with additional handicaps.

Religious affiliation: None

Maintained by: Royal National Institute for the Blind

Curriculum: The School aims to improve the pupils' quality of life, presenting educational challenges in a stimulating and caring environment. The curriculum focuses on visual development for the best use of sight; on physical development for control of the body; on social development for acceptable behaviour and individual personality; and on communication development to acquire expressive and receptive skills. A full 24 hour curriculum is available.

Entry requirements: Boys and girls with impaired visual function and developmental delay, with one or more additional handicaps. The School is particularly suitable for children needing individual intervention to acquire basic social, communication, physical and cognitive skills.

Staffing: A strong and qualified classroom and child care staff provides a pleasant and stimulating environment geared to meeting individual needs.

Academic and leisure facilities: The School has spacious classrooms with hydro-therapy and swimming pools, covered play area, sensory stimulation rooms and comfortable and homely residential quarters. Buildings are set in extensive grounds, and a wide range of leisure activities and trips is provided. Visits from parents are encouraged and parents' days are arranged when advice and support can be provided.

Royal National Institute for the Blind

PROSPECTUSES
MINI-PROSPECTUSES
NEWSLETTERS
EXHIBITION MATERIALS
MARKETING
VIDEO FILMS
SCHOOL MAGAZINES
SCHOOL YEAR BOOKS

John Catt Educational Limited

Great Glemham
Saxmundham
Suffolk IP17 2DH

Tel: 0728 78 666
Fax: 0728 78 415

JOHN CATT EDUCATIONAL LIMITED

RNIB Sunshine House Schools

(Founded 1919)

Southport, Merseyside
Northwood, Middlesex
East Grinstead, West Sussex

Age range: 2-8. Boarders from 2-8
No. of pupils enrolled as at 1.1.92:
The Schools take from 15-30 pupils
Range of fees per annum (incl VAT) as at 1.1.92 (payable by LEA):
Day: from £14,976
Boarding: from £22,467

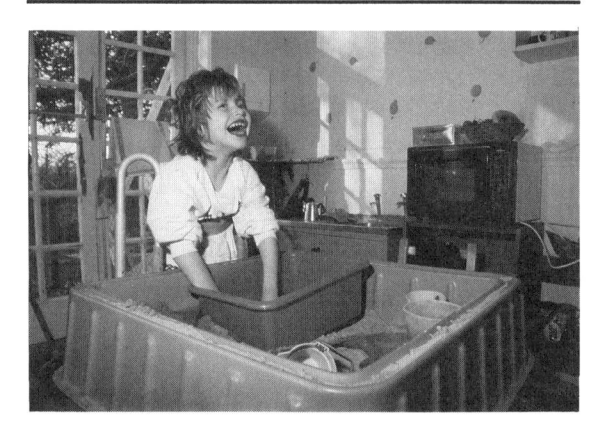

Type: Non-maintained special schools for visually handicapped boys and girls, many of whom have additional handicaps.

Religious affiliation: None

Maintained by: Royal National Institute for the Blind

Curriculum:
RNIB Sunshine House Schools meet the needs of young visually impaired children, many of whom have additional handicaps. Attendance patterns are flexible, and many pupils attend on a day or part-time basis. The schools aim for the maximum home-school contact.

Each child follows an individual teaching programme designed to develop communication skills, a knowledge of everyday things, individual independence, daily living skills and self confidence. A strong team of classroom and child care staff provides a pleasant and stimulating environment within which each child's particular needs are met.

Each school has well equipped classrooms and play areas, and comfortable, homely bedrooms for the children who board. A range of enjoyable activities is provided and visits from parents are encouraged.

For further details, please contact:-

Miss Helen Townend
Headteacher
RNIB Sunshine House School
2 Oxford Road
Birkdale
Southport
Merseyside PR8 2JT
Tel: 0704 67174

Mrs Maureen Walker
Headteacher
RNIB Sunshine House School
Dene Road
Northwood
Middlesex HA6 2DD
Tel: 0923 822538

Mr Michael Shaw
Headteacher
RNIB Sunshine House School
Dunnings Road
East Grinstead
West Sussex RH14 4ND
Tel: 0342 323141

Royal National Institute for the Blind

Authoritative articles covering many important aspects of Special Learning Needs appear at the start of the Guide. Parents are urged to read them.

Royal School for Deaf Children

(Founded 1792)

*Victoria Road, Margate,
Kent CT9 1NB
Tel: 0843 227561 Fax: 0843 227637*

Head: B.S. Armstrong
Age range: 4-19. Boarders from 4-19
No. of pupils enrolled as at 1.9.91: 167
Fees per annum:
Main School: Day £10,665, Boarding £17,489
Multiply Handicapped: Day £17,199, Boarding: £25,839
Further Education: £16,410

Type: Non-maintained Special School for deaf and multiply handicapped, deaf including deaf/blind

Religious denomination: All denominational

Member of: Non-maintained schools

Curriculum: A broad, balanced curriculum is provided by following the National Curriculum as far as is practicable in view of a child's individual needs and capabilities, with disapplication kept to a minimum and modification sensitively applied. Pupils with learning difficulties enjoy a strong practical element in their curriculum and in all Departments special attention is paid to the development of communication and to lifeskills.

Entry requirements: All children function as being severely to profoundly hearing impaired and require 'Total Communication'. Children may also have additional impairments.

Examinations offered: GCSE (Southern and ULEAC); City & Guilds, RSA, Pitmans.

Academic and leisure facilities: The School is extremely well equipped with special facilities for assessment, speech and language therapy, physiotherapy etc. Full range of leisure facilities including drama, sport including sailing.

Rutland House School

(Founded 1979)

*Elm Bank,
Mapperley,
Nottingham NG3 5AJ
Tel: 0602 621315 Fax: 0602 622867*

Headteacher: Mrs C A Oviatt-Ham
Age range: 2-19. Boarders from 2-19
No. of pupils enrolled as at 1.1.92: 25 (to be increased in 1992 - on two separate sites)
Junior: 10 Boys 7 Girls; Senior: 3 Boys 3 Girls
Sixth Form: 1 Boy 1 Girl
Fees per annum: Day: £19,196
Boarding: £31,977

Type: PMLD. All with Cerebral Palsy

Religious denomination: All

Member of: The Spastics Society

Curriculum: Children follow special programmes inspired by the work of the Peto Institute. All children have access to the National Curriculum through programmes of study.

Entry requirements: Children have cerebral palsy and special needs. All children are statemented for their special educational needs.

Academic and leisure facilities: Children belong to local Beavers, Cubs and Brownie groups. Children participate in Boccia. Children participate in many local events. Children have weekly exchanges with local Nursery and Primary Schools.

Don't forget to make use of the Reader Enquiry Service cards at the back of the Guide if you want more information about the Schools or Colleges listed.

St Rose's School

(Founded 1911)

*Stratford Lawn,
Stroud,
Gloucestershire GL5 4AB
Tel: 0453 763793*

Head: Sr M. Quentin, OP, BA
(Member of Dominican Order, NAHT)
Age range: 2-19. Boarders from 5
No. of pupils enrolled as at 1.1.92: 63
Junior: 22 Boys 14 Girls; Senior: 12 Boys 7 Girls
Sixth Form: 5 Boys 3 Girls
Fees per annum: Day: £13,237-£14,824
Boarding: £20,973-£23,490

Type: P.H. Children, who may also have Epilepsy, Speech and Language disorders, partially sighted or blind

Religious denomination: Roman Catholic, but all denominations welcome

Member of: NAIMS, NCSE

Curriculum: The curriculum includes all National Curriculum subjects, and GCSE is available for those who are able. For the less able a broad base curriculum is available to suit their needs - this would include Social Skills, Therapy, Creative Skills etc.

Entry requirements: All children have a physical disability which affects their learning to some degree and necessitates special or individual attention.

A full range of guides to UK Schools is also published by John Catt Educational.

Authoritative articles covering many important aspects of Special Learning Needs appear at the start of the Guide. Parents are urged to read them.

We specialise in consultancy, design, production and publication of:

- ☑ **Prospectuses**
- ☑ **Mini-prospectuses**
- ☑ **Newsletters**
- ☑ **Exhibition Materials**
- ☑ **Marketing**
- ☑ **Video Films**
- ☑ **School Magazines**
- ☑ **School Year Books**

Our experience and quality of craftsmanship enable us to give a service which we believe is unequalled by any other organisation at a highly competitive price.

For more details please telephone or write to:

John Catt Educational Limited
Great Glemham,
Saxmundham,
Suffolk IP17 2DH
Tel: 0728 78 666   Fax: 0728 78 415

St Vincent' School for the Visually Handicapped

(Founded 1841)

*Yew Tree Lane,
Liverpool L12 9HN
Tel: 051 228 9968 Fax: 051 252 0216*

Head: Sister Josephine Hawes
(Member of AEWVH)
Age range: 4-17. Boarders from 4-17
No. of pupils enrolled as at 1.1.92: 105
Junior: 23 Boys 13 Girls; Senior: 41 Boys 28 Girls
Fees per annum: Day: £11,058
Boarding: £16,044

Type: Non-maintained Special School for Blind and Partially Sighted Children

Religious denomination: Roman Catholic but takes any pupil

Member of: AEWVH, ICEVH

Curriculum: The full National Curriculum is available in both Primary and Secondary Departments. In addition pupils receive individual tuition in braille, mobility, the use of information technology, specially adapted to meet their needs and in life skills. As part of TVE, work experience is available for years 11 - 12. Teaching is ability based in small groups.

Entry requirements: Applications for admission come through Local Education Authorities who are then responsible for the fees. Parents are welcome to visit the School to see the facilities available.

Examinations offered: At GCSE level - English Language/Literature, Mathematics, Science, History, Geography, French, Music, Art, Child Care, Religious Education and Word Processing. AEB - World of Work, Life Skills, Health & Hygiene, English RSA and NPRA in a variety of subjects.

Academic and leisure facilities: The School is well equipped with modern technology for blind and partially sighted pupils with specialist teachers and rooms for all subjects. The highly experienced staff all hold additional qualifications as teachers of the Visually Handicapped. The School has a large gymnasium, heated indoor swimming pool, and soft play area. An attractive Youth Club offers a wide range of leisure interests, and use of local facilities are encouraged. The Duke of Edinburgh Scheme, Adventure Holidays, Guide Camps and trips abroad are regular features of school life.

Religious activities: Pupils of all religious

beliefs are welcome and are encouraged in the practise of their individual faith. The Roman Catholic ethos of the School ensures a happy Christian atmosphere.

Day and boarding places are available. Residential Accommodation is in six peer groups, all cared for by qualified House Parents.

Trengweath School

(Founded 1957)

*Hartley Road,
Plymouth PL1 5LW
Tel: 0752 771975 Fax: 0752 793388*

Head: Mrs J.A. Steward, BA, CertEd, SRN, SM, SRCN, HV
Age range: Diagnosis-12 years
No. of pupils enrolled as at 1.1.92: 24

Type: Boarding for young children with Cerebral Palsy, multiple physical disabilities, Sensory deprivation, some with additional frailty.

Religious denomination: Non-denominational

Curriculum: A broad relevant curriculum offering an holistic approach to delivery. Peto inspired work is also undertaken.

Vranch House School

(Founded 1969)

*Pinhoe Road,
Exeter EX4 8AD
Tel: 0392 68333*

Head: Mr S.C. Johnson, DipEd (PHC), FCollP
Age range: 2-12. Boarders from 5-12
No. of pupils enrolled as at 1.1.92: 40
32 Boys 8 Girls
Fees per annum: Day: £13,890
Boarding: £14,400

Type: Physically handicapped with other handicaps.

Religious denomination: Christian based, but non- denominational

Member of: NAIMS, Devon & Exeter Spastics Society

Curriculum: All children follow the National Curriculum, modified where necessary to meet their individual needs. Full treatment facilities are available (physiotherapy, hydrotherapy, speech therapy and occupational therapy). A "conductive learning" approach is used. Approved under the 1981 Education Act, a Registered Charity and a Company Limited by guarantee.

Entry requirements: Pupils are seen on a two-day admissions assessment and must be sponsored by an LEA unless private arrangements are made.

Academic and leisure facilities: The School has a 16 place hostel in pleasant rural countryside on the outskirts of Exeter. The School has a swimming/hydrotherapy pool. Two minibuses take children on excursions to nearby beaches and Dartmoor.

A full range of guides to UK Schools is also published by John Catt Educational.

Sensory & Physical Impairment
Colleges of Further Education

THE NATIONAL STAR CENTRE

College of Further Education

(Founded 1967)

Ullenwood,
Cheltenham,
Gloucestershire GL53 9QU
Tel: 0242 527631 Fax: 0242 222234

Principal: Allen Field, LCP, MRIPHH, FCollP
Age range: Post 16
No. of students enrolled as at 1.9.91:
Male: 63 Female: 38
Fees per annum: Resident Student: £17,910

Type: College of Further Education, Physical and Sensory Disabilities

Member of: Association of National Specialist Colleges

The College enables students who have a physical or sensory disability to follow a mainstream Further Education Curriculum, access to which is arranged on an individual student basis. Of equal importance is the intention that each student will be challenged and guided to develop the maximum personal independence. Together the abilities gained provide the essential requirements for a full integration into whatever area of society will then be the student's life.

Students aged from sixteen are accepted after an assessment interview which looks to see how the student may benefit from College provision and cope with the life of a busy college. Enrolment may be for one, two or three years and the course range offers General courses which combine studies across the subject range of the College with core studies aimed at determining one's own lifestyle and independence; wide ranging national prevocational certificate courses and recognised vocational courses in Business and Finance, Design, Leisure and Horticulture to NVQ Levels 1, 2 and 3. Examining Boards used include SEG, LEAC, AEB, City & Guilds, BTEC, RSA, Pitmans and LCC. Our supporting programme of work experience in the student's home area as well as our valued relationships with local employers has helped many on the road to a career.

The College enjoys purpose built facilities for both residence and education. The recently opened professional standard photography and design studios and the studio theatre join the carefully planned practical crafts and horticulture provision, the business and computer suites and office training area and extensive facilities which support the College's international sporting reputation.

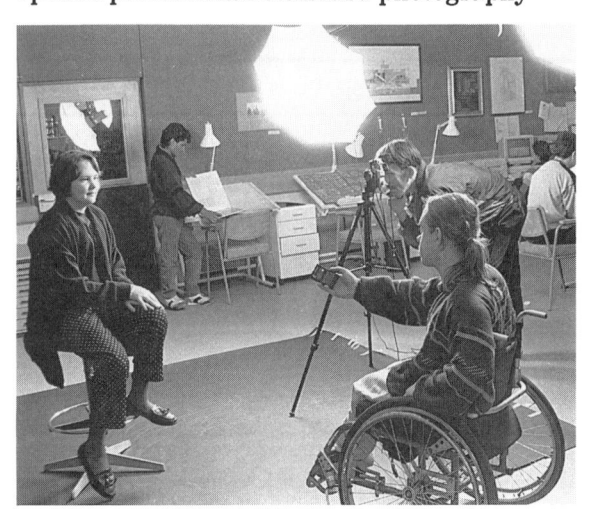

Residential accommodation is graded from the provision for total care through to fully independent accommodation in town and is supported by experienced medical and care staff. Physiotherapy, Speech Therapy and an individual communication aids service are all available as required.

The Student's Union, a range of clubs and societies, the opportunities in nearby Cheltenham, visits in this country and abroad help meet those leisure needs which in the end are perhaps best met by living life as a student away at College.

The Prospectus, course leaflets and a College video are available and informal visits may be arranged at any time. The College is recognised as efficient by the British Accreditation Council for Independent Further and Higher Education.

Don't forget to make use of the Reader Enquiry Service cards at the back of the Guide if you want more information about the Schools or Colleges listed.

Queen Elizabeth's Foundation for the Disabled

(Training College Established 1934)

*Woodlands Road,
Leatherhead,
Surrey KT22 0BN
Tel: 0372 842204 Fax: 0372 844072*

Head: (Banstead Place) A. Galt
Head: (Training College) J.S.P. Peake
Age range: 16 upwards. All residential.
Fees per annum:
Referrals from local authorities and disabled resettlement officers

Type: Banstead Place Assessment and Further Education Centre for young people with severe physical disabilities including brain injury. Queen Elizabeth's Training College - vocational training for jobs.

Banstead Place is a member of the National Association of Specialist Colleges and is accredited by the British Accreditation Council for Independent Further and Higher Education. Queen Elizabeth's Training

PORTLAND COLLEGE

Residential Training for People with Disabilities

Step onto the Ladder of Opportunity

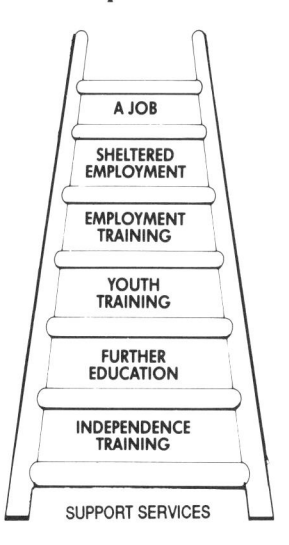

A JOB
SHELTERED EMPLOYMENT
EMPLOYMENT TRAINING
YOUTH TRAINING
FURTHER EDUCATION
INDEPENDENCE TRAINING
SUPPORT SERVICES

Assessment and Advice
Business Studies
Communication Skills
Computer Studies
Desktop Publishing
Electronics
Engineering
Foundation Skills
Head Injury Rehabilitation
Horology
Horticulture
Independent Living
Jobsearch
Life and Social Skills
Mobility
Numeracy and Literacy
Occupational Therapy
Physiotherapy
Prevocational Skills
Speech Therapy

For Information Contact
Julie Wilkes on (0623) 792141

Portland College
Nottingham Road
Mansfield
Nottinghamshire
NG18 4TJ

College is one of four Residential Training Colleges for people in the UK.

Curriculum: Banstead Place provides multi-disciplinary assessment and training for severely disabled young people, many of whom have learning difficulties.

Queen Elizabeth's Training College provides vocational training in 23 professions, both commercial and technical.

Entry requirements: For information concerning entry requirements, contact the Foundation on 0372 842204.

RNIB Hethersett College

(Founded 1956)

Philanthropic Road, Redhill, Surrey RH1 4DZ
Tel: 0737 768935 Fax: 0737 765907

Head: Dr M. Rowe, PhD, MSc, DLC, MIBiol
Age range: 16+. Boarders from 16+
No. of pupils enrolled as at 1.1.92: 98
Fees per annum: Day: £13,365 - £14,412
Boarding: £21,000 - £24,000

Type: College of Further Education and Vocational Training for the visually impaired

Member of: NATSPEC (National Association of Specialist Colleges)

Curriculum: The College offers four types of course: Life Skills; Foundation Course; Pre-Vocational Education (CPVE); Vocational Training Courses.

Entry requirements: All students are visually impaired. Many have additional disabilities/needs. Entry according to individual assessment and interview.

Royal National Institute for the Blind

Directory of Schools specialising in Learning Difficulties

Avon

ST CHRISTOPHERS SCHOOL
2 Carisbrooke Lodge, Westbury Park, Avon BS6 7JE
Tel: (0272) 733301
Head: Miss H Murray
Type: Co-educational Boarding & Day 6-19
No of pupils: B29 G26 No of boarders 54
Special Needs: EBD PH SLD SMH
Independent

THE SHEILING SCHOOL
Thornbury Park, Avon BS12 1HP
Tel: (0454) 412194
Type: Co-educational Boarding 6-16
No of pupils: B26 G25 No of boarders 51
Special Needs: DYS EBD MH MLD SLD SMH SpD SpL
Independent

Berkshire

ANNIE LAWSON SCHOOL
Nine Mile Ride, Ravenswood Village, Crowthorne, Berkshire RG11 6BQ
Tel: (0344) 771212
Head: Ms A MacNaughton
Type: Co-educational Boarding & Day 5-19
No of pupils: 50
Special Needs: Bl D PH VIS
Approved Independent

Buckinghamshire

MACINTYRE SCHOOL
The Old Manor House, Wingrave, Aylesbury, Buckinghamshire HP22 4PD
Tel: (0296) 681274/681657
Head: Mrs J Wadhams
Type: Co-educational Boarding & Day 5-19
No of pupils: B22 G20 No of boarders 42
Special Needs: AUT SLD SMH
Approved Independent

Cheshire

THE DAVID LEWIS SCHOOL
Mill Lane, Warford, Cheshire SK9 7UD
Tel: (0565) 872613
Head: Mrs S Harte
Type: Co-educational Boarding & Day 5-19
No of pupils: B50 G29 No of boarders 78
Special Needs: EBD EPI MH MLD PH SLD SMH SpD
Non - maintained

THE ST JOHN VIANNEY SCHOOL
(Lower School), Didsbury Road, Heaton Mersey, Stockport, Cheshire SK4 2AA
Tel: (061) 432 0510
Head: M J Lochery
Type: Co-educational Day 5-11
Special Needs: EBD SpD
Non - maintained

Devon

BRADFIELD HOUSE SCHOOL
Willand, Cullompton, Devon EX15 2QY
Tel: (0884) 33462
Head: S R Jones
Type: Boys Boarding & Day 11-17
No of pupils: 60 No of boarders 55
Special Needs: DYS EBD MLD SpL
Approved Independent

BROOMHAYES SCHOOL
78 Atlantic Way, Northam, Devon EX39 1JQ
Tel: (0237) 473830
Head: Mrs W Brown
Type: Co-educational Boarding & Day 10-19
No of pupils: 20 No of boarders 19
Special Needs: AUT EBD MH MLD SLD SMH SpD SpL
Approved Independent

Dorset

BOVERIDGE HOUSE
Cranborne, Wimborne, Dorset BH21 5RV
Tel: (07254) 218
Head: Miss P Harper
Type: Co-educational Boarding & Day 7-18
No of pupils: B35 G35 No of boarders 68
Special Needs: EBD MLD SpD SpL
Approved Independent

PORTFIELD SCHOOL
14 Stour Road, Christchurch, Dorset BH23 1PS
Tel: (0202) 486626
Head: Mrs P Thomas
Type: Co-educational Boarding & Day 5-19
No of pupils: B24 G6 No of boarders 17
Special Needs: AUT
Approved Independent

WOODSFORD HOUSE
Woodsford, Nr Dorchester, Dorset DT2 8AT
Tel: (0305) 848202
Head: Mr & Mrs R S R Mileham
Type: Co-educational Boarding & Day 7-13
No of pupils: B23 G5 No of boarders 23
Special Needs: DYS
Independent

Essex

DOUCECROFT SCHOOL
163 High Street, Kelvedon, Colchester, Essex CO5 9JA
Tel: (0376) 570060
Head: Kathy Cranmer
Type: Co-educational Boarding & Day 3-19
No of pupils: B14 G7 No of weekly boarders 12
Special Needs: AUT
Approved Independent

GREAT STONEY SCHOOL
Ongar, Essex CM5 OAD
Tel: (0277) 362027
Head: C Tombs
Type: Co-educational Boarding 7-19
No of pupils: B70 G30 No of boarders 100
Non - maintained

WOODCROFT SCHOOL
Whitakers Way, Loughton, Essex IG10 1SQ
Tel: (081) 508 1369
Head: B R Edwards
Type: Co-educational Day 2-11 *No of pupils:* B9 G9
Special Needs: AUT BI EBD EPI MH MLD PH PHe SLD SMH SpD SpL VIS
Approved Independent

Hampshire

HOPE LODGE SCHOOL
41 Belmont Road, Portswood, Southampton, Hampshire SO2 1GD
Tel: (0703) 554729
Head: Mrs M E Rigg
Type: Co-educational Boarding & Day 4-16
No of pupils: B22 G5 No of weekly boarders 16
Special Needs: AUT SLD
Approved Independent

THE SHEILING CURATIVE SCHOOLS
Ashley, Ringwood, Hampshire BH24 2EB
Tel: (04254) 477488
Head: Dr L Sahlmann
Type: Co-educational Boarding & Day 6-16
No of pupils: B30 G13 No of boarders 43
Special Needs: MH MLD SLD
Independent

Hereford & Worcester

BESFORD COURT SCHOOL
Ladywood Road, Besford, Worcester WR8 9AQ
Tel: (0386) 552074
Head: P Quigley
Type: Co-educational Boarding & Day 8-16
No of pupils: B50 G15 No of boarders 65
Special Needs: EBD MH MLD SLD SpD SpL
Non - maintained

GRANGE HOUSE SCHOOL
Lucton, Leominster, Hereford & Worcester HR6 9PJ
Tel: (056885) 466
Head: Mrs A Harner
Type: Co-educational Boarding & Day 6-17
No of pupils: B70 G15 No of boarders 35
Special Needs: DYS
Approved Independent

KINLOSS SCHOOL
Martley, Worcester WR6 6QB
Tel: (0886) 888223
Head: D Tuohy
Type: Boys Boarding & Day 10-17
No of pupils: 65 No of boarders 62
Special Needs: DYS
Approved Independent

ROWDEN HOUSE SCHOOL
Rowden House, Winslow, Bromyard, Hereford & Worcester HR7 4LS
Tel: (0885) 488096
Head: Mrs J Leach
Type: Co-educational Boarding 11-19
No of pupils: 25 No of boarders 25
Special Needs: EBD SLD
Approved Independent

Kent

BOURNE PLACE SCHOOL
Nizels Lane, Hildenborough, Tonbridge, Kent TN11 8NS
Tel: (0732) 832666
Head: G Davies
Type: Co-educational Boarding & Day 8-19
No of pupils: B51 G13 No of boarders 64
Special Needs: EBD MLD SpL
Non - maintained

EAST COURT
Victoria Parade, Ramsgate, Kent CT11 8ED
Tel: (0843) 592077
Head: Dr M Thomson & E J Watkins
Type: Co-educational Boarding & Day 8-13
No of pupils: B60 G8 No of boarders 57
Special Needs: DYS SLD
Approved Independent

HELEN ALLISON SCHOOL
Longfield Road, Meopham, Kent DA13 OEW
Tel: (0474) 814878
Head: Miss L Marshall
Type: Co-educational Boarding & Day 5-19
No of pupils: B38 G7 No of boarders 28
Special Needs: AUT
Approved Independent

Lancashire

CROWTHORN SCHOOL
Broadhead Road, Turton, Bolton, Lancashire BL7 OJS
Tel: (0204) 852143
Head: S Forster
Type: Co-educational Boarding & Day 7-16
No of pupils: B50 G36 No of boarders 86
Special Needs: EBD MLD
Non - maintained

PETERHOUSE SCHOOL FOR AUTISTIC CHILDREN
32 Chambres Road, Southport, Lancashire PR8 6JQ
Tel: (0704) 532519
Head: Ms B Hatton
Type: Co-educational Boarding & Day 5-19
No of pupils: B23 G3 No of boarders 24
Special Needs: AUT MH
Approved Independent

PONTVILLE SCHOOL
Blackmoss Lane, Ormskirk, Lancashire L39 4TW
Tel: (0695) 578734
Head: Sister E Dawson
Type: Co-educational Boarding & Day 9-19
No of pupils: B40 G30 No of boarders 55
Special Needs: EBD MH MLD PHe SpD VIS
Non - maintained

Lincolnshire

KISIMUL SCHOOL
The Old Vicarage, Swinderby, Lincoln, LN6 9LU
Tel: (0522) 279
Head: Mr & Mrs H B Matthews
Type: Co-educational Boarding 9-19
No of pupils: B16 G6 No of boarders 22
Special Needs: AUT EBD EPI MH MLD PHe SLD SMH SpD
Approved Independent

London

CENTER ACADEMY
Napier Hall, Hide Place, Vincent Square, London SW1P 4NJ
Tel: (071) 821 5760/5627
Head: R Detweiler
Type: Co-educational Day 5-18 *No of pupils:* B41 G9
Special Needs: DYS MLD SLD SpL
Independent

FAIRLEY HOUSE SCHOOL
44 Bark Place, London W2 4AT
Tel: (071) 229 0977
Head: Mrs P Thomson
Type: Co-educational Day 5-11 *No of pupils:* B72 G16
Special Needs: DYS
Independent

HAMPSTEAD INTERNATIONAL SCHOOL
16 Netherhall Gardens, London NW3 5TJ
Tel: (071) 794 0018
Head: Ms L Winch
Type: Co-educational Day 3-19
Special Needs: MLD
Independent

HELEN ARKELL DYSLEXIA CENTRE
The Hornsby Centre School,
71 Wandsworth Common Westside,
London SW18 2ED
Tel: (081) 871 2846
Head: Dr B Hornsby
Type: Co-educational Day 3-11
No of pupils: B74 G70
Special Needs: DYS MLD SpD SpL
Approved Independent

KISHARON SCHOOL
1011 Finchley Road, London NW11 7HB
Tel: (081) 455 7483
Head: Mrs C Lehman
Type: Co-educational Day 2-13
No of pupils: B16 G5
Special Needs: MH MLD
Approved Independent

PARAYHOUSE SCHOOL
St John's, World's End, King's Road,
London SW10 0LU
Tel: (071) 352 2882
Head: Mrs S L Jackson
Type: Co-educational Day 4-18
No of pupils: B26 G25
Special Needs: AUT EBD MLD PH PHe SpD SpL VIS
Independent

THE SYBIL ELGAR SCHOOL
10 Florence Road, London W5 3TX
Tel: (081) 567 9844
Head: R Marsh
Type: Co-educational Boarding & Day 4-19
No of pupils: 27
Special Needs: AUT
Approved Independent

Greater Manchester

THE ST JOHN VIANNEY SCHOOL
(Upper School),
Rye Bank Road, Firswood, Stretford,
Greater Manchester M16
Tel: (061) 881 7843
Head: M J Lochery
Type: Co-educational Day 11-16
Special Needs: EBD SpD
Non - maintained

Merseyside

WARGRAVE HOUSE SCHOOL FOR AUTISTIC CHILDREN
Wargrave Road, Newton-le-Willows, Merseyside WA12 8RS
Tel: (0925) 224899
Head: Mrs P M Maddock
Type: Co-educational Boarding & Day 4-19
No of pupils: B24 G8 No of weekly boarders 20
Special Needs: AUT
Approved Independent

Middlesex

PIELD HEATH SCHOOL
Pield Heath Road, Uxbridge, Middlesex UB8 3NW
Tel: (0895) 258507/233092
Head: Sister Julie Rose
Type: Co-educational Boarding & Day 7-19
No of pupils: 100 No of boarders 60
Special Needs: MLD PHe SLD SpD SpL
Non - maintained

Norfolk

REEVES HALL SCHOOL
Hepworth, Diss, Norfolk IP22 2PP
Tel: (0359) 50217
Head: Mrs J P Richards
Type: Co-educational Boarding & Day 9-17
No of pupils: B16 G7 No of boarders 23
Special Needs: DYS
Approved Independent

Northumberland

NUNNYKIRK HALL SCHOOL
Netherwitton, Morpeth, Northumberland NE61 4PB
Tel: (0670) 72685
Head: P R A Booker
Type: Co-educational Boarding & Day 9-16+
No of pupils: B31 G9 No of boarders 40
Special Needs: DYS EBD SpL
Approved Independent

Nottinghamshire

DAWN HOUSE SCHOOL
Helmsley Road, Rainworth, Mansfield, Nottinghamshire NG21 0DQ
Tel: (0623) 795361
Head: Miss S Richmond
Type: Co-educational Boarding & Day 5-16
No of pupils: B69 G15 No of boarders 59
Special Needs: SpD
Non - maintained

SUTHERLAND HOUSE SCHOOL (PRIMARY DEPARTMENT)
Sutherland Road, Nottingham NG3 7AP
Tel: (0602) 873375
Head: Maria Allen
Type: Co-educational Day 3-11
No of pupils: 30
Special Needs: AUT
Approved Independent

SUTHERLAND HOUSE SCHOOL (SECONDARY DEPARTMENT)
'Westward', 68 Cyprus Road, Mapperley Park, Nottinghamshire
Tel: (0602) 691823
Head: Coral Byles
Type: Co-educational Day 11-16
No of pupils: 12
Special Needs: AUT
Approved Independent

Shropshire

LOPPINGTON HOUSE FURTHER EDUCATION & ADULT CENTRE
Loppington, Wem, Shropshire SY4 5NF
Tel: (0939) 33926
Head: P Harris
Type: Co-educational 16-19
Special Needs: BI EBD EPI PH SLD

OVERLEY HALL SCHOOL
Wellington, Telford, Shropshire TF6 5HD
Tel: (0952) 86262
Head: Mrs V E Trussler
Type: Co-educational Boarding & Day 9-19
No of pupils: 22
Special Needs: AUT CP EBD EPI MH MLD PH SLD SMH SpD SpL VIS
Approved Independent

QUEEN'S PARK SCHOOL DYSLEXIA CENTRE
Queen's Park, Oswestry, Shropshire SY11 2HZ
Tel: (0691) 652416
Head: Mrs D Baur
Type: Co-educational Boarding & Day B8-13 G8-16
Special Needs: DYS SpL
Independent

Somerset

EDINGTON SCHOOL
Mark Road, Burtle, Bridgwater, Somerset TA7 8NJ
Tel: (0278) 722012
Head: G L Nickerson
Type: Co-educational Boarding & Day 8-13
No of pupils: B104 G6 No of boarders 71
Special Needs: DYS
Non - maintained

MARK COLLEGE
Mark, Highbridge, Somerset TA9 4NP
Tel: (0278) 64632
Head: Dr S J Chinn
Type: Boys Boarding & Day 11-16
No of pupils: 80 No of boarders 75
Special Needs: DYS
Approved Independent

SHAPWICK SENIOR SCHOOL
Shapwick Manor, Shapwick, Bridgwater, Somerset TA7 9NJ
Tel: (0458) 210384
Head: D C Walker & J P Whittock
Type: Co-educational Boarding & Day 13-17
No of pupils: B96 G3 No of boarders 84
Special Needs: DYS
Approved Independent

Staffordshire

MAPLE HAYES HALL
Abnalls Lane, Litchfield, Staffordshire WV13 8BL
Tel: (0543) 264387
Head: Dr E Neville Brown
Type: Boys Boarding & Day 7-17
No of pupils: 120 No of boarders 88
Special Needs: DYS SpL
Approved Independent

Suffolk

ELLOUGH SCHOOL
The Grange, Church Road, Ellough, Beccles, Suffolk NR34 7TR
Tel: (0502) 711739
Head: C G Stewart
Type: Co-educational Boarding & Day 7-13
No of pupils: 75
Special Needs: DYS
Independent

MOATS TYE SCHOOL
Moats Tye, Stowmarket, Suffolk IP14 2EY
Tel: (0449) 613358
Head: Mrs J B Emmett & Mrs P M Oliver
Type: Co-educational Day 6-10
No of pupils: B10 G10
Special Needs: DYS
Approved Independent

THE OLD RECTORY
Brettenham, Ipswich, Suffolk
Tel: (0449) 736404
Head: M A Phillips
Type: Co-educational Boarding & Day 7-13
No of pupils: B37 G8 No of boarders 40
Special Needs: DYS SpL
Approved Independent

Surrey

KEFFOLDS FARMS TUTORIAL SCHOOL
Keffolds Farm, Bunch Lane, Haslemere, Surrey GU8 4DX
Tel: (0428) 642718
Head: J M E Foord
Type: Co-educational Boarding & Day 7-13
No of pupils: B15 G13 No of boarders 18
Special Needs: DYS MLD
Approved Independent

THE KNOWL HILL SCHOOL
School Lane, Pirbright, Surrey GU24 OJN
Tel: (0483) 797032
Head: Mrs A J Bareford & Mrs J Schiller
Type: Co-educational Boarding & Day 7-16
No of pupils: B20 G5 No of boarders 8
Special Needs: DYS
Independent

THE LINK DAY PRIMARY SCHOOL
138 Croydon Road, Beddington, Croydon, Surrey CR0 4PG
Tel: (081) 688 5239
Head: Mrs F Tomlin
Type: Co-educational Day 6-12
No of pupils: 35
Special Needs: DYS SpD SpL
Approved Independent

THE LINK SECONDARY SCHOOL
82-84 Croydon Road, Bedington, Surrey CRO 4PD
Tel: (081) 688 7691
Head: W E Fuller
Type: Co-educational Day 11-17
No of pupils: B26 G8
Special Needs: DYS SpD SpL
Approved Independent

MEATH SCHOOL
Brox Road, Ottershaw, Surrey KT16 0LF
Tel: (0932) 872302
Head: Mrs G Hart
Type: Co-educational Boarding & Day 5-12
No of pupils: 76 No of boarders 46
Special Needs: EBD MLD SpD SpL
Non - maintained

MORE HOUSE SCHOOL
Frensham, Farnham, Surrey GU10 3AW
Tel: (025025) 2303
Head: S M Mullen
Type: Boys Boarding & Day 10-17
No of pupils: 108 No of boarders 78
Special Needs: DYS EBD MLD
Approved Independent

RUTHERFORDS SCHOOL
1A Melville Avenue, South Croydon,
Surrey CR2 7HZ
Tel: (081) 688 7560
Head: Mrs P Netley
Type: Co-educational Day 2-12
No of pupils: 24
Special Needs: PH PHe SMH SpD SpL VIS
Approved Independent

ST JOSEPH'S SCHOOL
Amlets Lane, Cranleigh, Surrey GU6 7NQ
Tel: (0483) 272449
Head: A Lowry
Type: Co-educational Boarding & Day 5-19
No of pupils: B60 G10 No of boarders 63
Special Needs: MLD SLD SpD
Non - maintained

ST MARGARET'S SCHOOL
Tadworth Court, Tadworth,
Surrey KT20 5RU
Tel: (0737) 357171
Head: Mrs A O'Connor
Type: Co-educational Boarding 8-19
No of pupils: 34 No of boarders 30
Special Needs: Bl D PH PHe SLD SMH VIS
Approved Independent

ST PIERS LINGFIELD
St Pier's Lane, Lingfield, Surrey RH7 6PW
Tel: (0342) 832243
Head: Mrs A Hurling
Type: Co-educational Boarding & Day 5-19
No of pupils: B155 G77 No of boarders 226
Special Needs: EBD EPI MH MLD PHe SLD SpD SpL VIS
Non - maintained

East Sussex

BRICKWALL HOUSE
Northiam, Rye, East Sussex TN31 6NL
Tel: (0797) 252494
Head: The Revd A B Fiddian-Green
Type: Boys Boarding & Day 10-17
No of pupils: 100 No of boarders 90
Special Needs: DYS
Approved Independent

HAWKHURST COURT DYSLEXIA CENTRE
Brighton College, 161 Eastern Road, Brighton,
East Sussex BN2 2AG
Tel: (0273) 681484
Head: Mrs M F Hollinshead
Type: Co-educational Boarding & Day 7-13
No of pupils: B40 G6 No of boarders 19
Special Needs: DYS SpL
Independent

HOLLY HOUSE
Beaconsfield Road, Chelwood Gate, East Sussex RH17 7LF
Tel: (0825) 740484
Head: Mrs D A Birchell
Type: Co-educational Boarding & Day 5-12
No of pupils: B8 G8 No of boarders 16
Special Needs: DYS EBD MLD PHe SpD SpL
Independent

NORTHEASE MANOR
Rodmell, Lewes, East Sussex BN7 3EJ
Tel: (0273) 472915
Head: R J Dennien
Type: Co-educational Boarding & Day 10-18
No of pupils: B80 G16 No of weekly boarders 74
Special Needs: DYS SpL
Approved Independent

OWLSWICK SCHOOL
Newhaven Road, Kingston, Lewes, East Sussex BN7 3PL
Tel: (0273) 473078
Heads: Mr & Mrs A K Harper
Type: Co-educational Boarding 9-18
No of pupils: B7 G4 No of boarders 11
Special Needs: EBD MLD
Approved Independent

ST JOHN'S RESIDENTIAL SCHOOL
Walpole Road, Brighton, East Sussex BN2 2AF
Tel: (0273) 570795
Head: A D Forster
Type: Co-educational Boarding 6-19
No of pupils: B52 G28 No of boarders 80
Special Needs: EBD MLD SLD SpD SpL
Non - maintained

West Sussex

THE JOHN HORNIMAN SCHOOL
2 Park Road, Worthing, West Sussex BN11 2AS
Tel: (0903) 200317
Head: Ms J Dunn
Type: Co-educational Boarding & Day 5-10
No of pupils: B15 G15 No of boarders 24
Special Needs: SpD SpL
Non - maintained

Tyne and Wear

TYNE AND WEAR AUTISTIC SOCIETY
Thornhill Park School, 21 Thornhill Park, Sunderland,
Tyne and Wear SR2 7LA
Tel: (091) 514 0659
Head: Mrs S F Ramm
Type: Co-educational Boarding & Day 2-19
No of pupils: 78 No of boarders 46
Special Needs: AUT
Approved Independent

West Midlands

SUNFIELD CHILDRENS HOMES
Clent, Stourbridge, West Midlands DY9 9PB
Tel: (0562) 882253
Head: R W Brocklebank
Type: Co-educational Boarding 6-19
No of pupils: B72 G38 No of boarders 110
Special Needs: EBD MH SLD SMH
Approved Independent

North Yorkshire

EXTENDED EDUCATION UNIT
Ian Tetley Memorial School, Lund Lane, Killinghall, Harrogate, North Yorkshire
Tel: (0423) 567258
Head: R P Richardson
Type: Co-educational Boarding 16-19
No of pupils: 30 No of boarders 30
Special Needs: MH MLD PH PHe SLD SpD SpL
Non - maintained

IAN TETLEY MEMORIAL SCHOOL
Lund Lane, Killinghall, Harrogate, North Yorkshire HG3 2BP7
Tel: (0423) 567258
Head: R P Richardson
Type: Co-educational Boarding & Day 4-19
No of pupils: 50 No of boarders 30
Special Needs: MH MLD PH PHe SLD SpD SpL
Non - maintained

South Yorkshire

FULLERTON HOUSE SCHOOL
off Tickhill Square, Denaby, Doncaster, South Yorkshire DN12 4AR
Tel: (0709) 861663
Head: I Archer
Type: Co-educational Boarding 8-19
No of pupils: 25 No of boarders 25
Special Needs: SLD SMH SpD SpL VIS
Approved Independent

STORM HOUSE SCHOOL
134 Barnsley Road, Wath upon Dearne, South Yorkshire S63 6OZ
Tel: (0709) 874443
Head: Mrs J Collins
Type: Co-educational Boarding & Day 4-19
No of pupils: 31 No of boarders 14
Special Needs: SLD
Approved Independent

SCOTLAND

Aberdeenshire

LINN MOOR RESIDENTIAL SCHOOL
Peterculter, Aberdeenshire AB1 0PJ
Tel: (0224) 732246
Head: Dr R Jackson
Type: Co-educational Boarding 5-18
No of pupils: B23 G8 No of boarders 31
Special Needs: AUT EBD MLD SLD SMH SpD
Approved Independent

Clackmannanshire

STRUAN HOUSE SCHOOL
27 Claremont, Alloa, Clackmannanshire FK10 2DG
Tel: (0259) 213435
Head: J Taylor
Type: Co-educational Boarding & Day 5-16
No of pupils: B20 G4 No of weekly boarders 22
Special Needs: AUT

Fife

LENDRICK MUIR SCHOOL
Rumbling Bridge, Kinross, Fife KY13 7PZ
Tel: (05774) 258
Head: R W Hayles
Type: Co-educational Boarding & Day 8-18
No of pupils: B50 G15 No of boarders 40
Special Needs: DYS
Approved Independent

Glasgow

EAST PARK HOME SCHOOL
1092 Maryhill Road, Glasgow G20 9TD
Tel: (041) 946 8315
Head: Mrs C M Leggate
Type: Co-educational Boarding & Day 2-19
No of pupils: B27 G15 No of boarders 38
Special Needs: PH PHe SLD SpD VIS

Kincardineshire

TEMPLEHILL COMMUNITY SCHOOL
Glenfarquhar Lodge, Laurencekirk, Kincardineshire AB30 1UJ
Tel: (056) 12230
Head: G Bell
Type: Co-educational Boarding 16-25
No of pupils: B21 G10 No of boarders 31
Special Needs: SMH
Independent

Peeblesshire

GARVALD SCHOOL AND TRAINING CENTRE
Dolphinton, West Linton, Peeblesshire EH46 7HJ
Tel: (0968) 82211
Head: M Dawson
Type: Co-educational Boarding 16-25
No of pupils: B22 G10 No of boarders 32
Special Needs: EBD MH MLD SLD SpD SpL

Stirling

CAMPHILL BLAIR DRUMMOND TRUST
Blair Drummond House, By Stirling, Stirling FK9 4UT
Tel: (0786) 841341
Head: Mr and Mrs G Schad
Type: Co-educational Boarding & Day 16-19
No of pupils: B7 G6 No of boarders 12
Special Needs: EBD MH MLD SLD SpD
Approved Independent

WALES

South Glamorgan

NCH HEADLANDS SCHOOL
Paget Place, Penarth, South Glamorgan CF6 1YY
Tel: (0222) 709771/2
Head: P Carradice
Type: Co-educational Boarding & Day 10-17
No of pupils: B30 G10 No of boarders 40
Special Needs: EBD MLD SLD
Approved Independent

Display Listings of Schools specialising in Learning Difficulties

Boveridge House School

(Founded: DES approved 1984)

*Cranborne,
Wimborne,
Dorset BH21 5RU
Tel: 07254 218*

Head: Miss P Harper
Age range: 8-19. Boarders from 8
No. of pupils enrolled as at 1.9.91: 63
29 Boys   34 Girls
Fees per annum: Day: £1540, Boarding £3355

Type: School for children with learning difficulties and related medical problems

Curriculum: The school follows a modified GCSE school curriculum.

Entry requirements: By interview.

We specialise in consultancy, design, production and publication of:

- ☑ **Prospectuses**
- ☑ **Mini-prospectuses**
- ☑ **Newsletters**
- ☑ **Exhibition Materials**
- ☑ **Marketing**
- ☑ **Video Films**
- ☑ **School Magazines**
- ☑ **School Year Books**

Our experience and quality of craftsmanship enable us to give a service which we believe is unequalled by any other organisation at a highly competitive price.

John Catt Educational Limited
Great Glemham,
Saxmundham,
Suffolk IP17 2DH
Tel: 0728 78 666   Fax: 0728 78 415

Brickwall School

(Founded 1930)

From Sept 1992 to be known as
Frewen College

*Brickwall House, Northian
Northiam,
Nr. Rye,
East Sussex TN31 6NL
Tel: 0797 252494 Fax: 0797 252567*

Principal: A.B. Fiddian-Green, MA, CertEd
Age range of pupils: 10-17. Boarders from 10
No. of pupils enrolled as at 1.9.91: 100
Fees per term: Day: £2300, Boarding £4700

Type: Boarding School (Specific Needs - Dyslexia only)

Curriculum: Modified curriculum for dyslexic boys. We follow the National Curriculum demands.

Entry requirements and procedures: Educational Psychologist's report and interview.

17th Century house plus 100 acres. Seven miles north west of Rye. Two Houses plus new classroom blocks. Excellent GCSE courses. Evening/weekend activities.

Normal curriculum schools with facilities to help pupils with Dyslexia or Special Learning Needs appear in Section Four.

Center Academy

(Founded 1974)

*Napier Hall, Hide Place,
Vincent Square, London SW1P 4NJ
Tel: (071) 821 5760 Fax: (071) 233 6337*

Head: Dr Robert E. Detweiler, JD
Age range: 7 - 18
No. of pupils enrolled as at 1.5.91:
Lower: 8 Boys 2 Girls; Middle: 12 Boys 3 Girls
Upper: 27 Boys 3 Girls
Fees per annum: Day: £6700-£7100

Type: School for children with Learning Difficulties

Member of: European Council of International Schools, London International Schools Association, British Dyslexia Association

Curriculum: Center Academy is a full day school for children with learning difficulties such as dyslexia. Our students have normal or above intelligence, but they demonstrate specific deficiencies because of problems with motivation, maturing or learning. While teaching them how to overcome their learning difficulties we also teach standard curriculum content so that they can stay abreast of their peers. Older students are preparing for GCSEs or American high school graduation. There is a complete activities and athletic programme.

Entry requirements: Admission is by evaluation of ability, learning style and achievement levels done at the school. Information and Prospectus available upon request.

Crowthorn School

(Founded 1872)

*Broadhead Road,
Edgworth, Turton,
Bolton, Lancashire BL7 0JS
Tel: 0204 852143*

Head: Mr Stan Forster, DAES, SCRCCYP, F(Coll)P
Age range: 7-16+. Boarders from 7
No. of pupils enrolled as at 1.1.92: 80
Junior: 25 Boys 5 Girls; Senior: 35 Boys 15 Girls
Fees per annum:
Termly Boarding: £22,500; 52 week care: £29,500

Type: Moderate learning difficulties (MLD)/Emotional Behavioural Difficulties (EBD)

Religious denomination: Methodist

Member of: The National Children's Home (NCH)

Curriculum: The School is committed to delivering the whole range of National Curriculum subjects wherever this is appropriate to the individual needs of our pupils. This is met through use of a modular approach which also allows for programmes to be tailored to the particular attainment level of each child.

Entry requirements: There are no formal entry requirements. Each case will be considered separately.

Examinations offered: A profile of a child's progress through the school is maintained by means of a Records of Achievement File. These records, based on our modular curriculum approach are gradually being validated by NPRA (The Northern Partnership of Records of Achievement).

Academic and leisure facilities: The School

forms a village community with residential accommodation being provided in nine residential groups separate from the classrooms. All work areas are well equipped and there are specialist facilities for science, art, craft and pottery, photography, CDT, and music. There is also a heated indoor swimming pool, a gymnasium and large sports hall, used by both pupils of Crowthorn and members of the local community.

Don't forget to make use of the Reader Enquiry Service cards at the back of the Guide if you want more information about the Schools or Colleges listed.

We specialise in consultancy, design, production and publication of:

- ☑ **Prospectuses**
- ☑ **Mini-prospectuses**
- ☑ **Newsletters**
- ☑ **Exhibition Materials**
- ☑ **Marketing**
- ☑ **Video Films**
- ☑ **School Magazines**
- ☑ **School Year Books**

Our experience and quality of craftsmanship enable us to give a service which we believe is unequalled by any other organisation at a highly competitive price.

John Catt Educational Limited
Great Glemham,
Saxmundham,
Suffolk IP17 2DH
Tel: 0728 78 666   Fax: 0728 78 415

Dawn House School

(Founded 1974)

*Helmsley Road,
Rainworth,
Nottinghamshire NG21 0DQ
Tel: 0623 795361*

Head: Mr A. Large, BA(Hons), MSc
Age range: 5-16
No. of pupils enrolled as at 1.1.92: 94
Junior: 52 Boys 11 Girls; Senior: 25 Boys 6 Girls
Fees per annum: LEAs should apply to ICAN for current day or boarding fees

Type: Non-maintained special day and boarding school for pupils with severe specific speech and language impairment.

Administered by a national charity: Invalid Children's Aid Nationwide (ICAN), 10 Bowling Green Lane, London EC1R 0BD

Curriculum: The school provides a broad and balanced curriculum, at an appropriate language level, within National Curriculum guidelines. Excellent facilities, together with an experienced and highly qualified multi-disciplinary staff team mean that specialist subjects and speech/language therapy are available, linked with a consistent and caring out-of-school environment.

Entry requirements: Pupils are within the average range of non-verbal ability, with a primary speech or language difficulty. Referral may be made by a local Education Authority when intensive speech and language therapy provision, allied to a carefully structured teaching programme, in a relevant small group setting, is not available locally.

An *'I CAN'* School
for Children with
Specific Speech and Language Impairment

Fairley House School

(Founded 1982)

*44 Bark Place,
London W2 4AT
Tel: 071 229 0977*

Principal: Mrs Patience Thomson, MA, MEd
Age range: 5-11+
No. of pupils enrolled as at 1.1.92: 88
72 Boys 16 Girls
Fees per annum: £9750

Type: Day School for children with Specific Learning Difficulties (Dyslexia)

Religious denomination: Inter-denominational

Curriculum: The prime aim is to improve the basic literacy and numeracy skills and to establish the self-confidence of dyslexic children. There is a 1:3 staff/pupil ratio with small group and individual remedial teaching and a structured, multi-sensory approach. The National Curriculum is followed throughout the School with emphasis on IT, Science and CDT. Children normally remain for 2-3 years and are carefully prepared for appropriate onward placement.

Entry requirements: Fairley House School Assessment.

Grange House School

(Founded 1987)

*Lucton,
Leominster,
Herefordshire HR6 9PJ
Tel: 056 885 466*

Head: Mrs Ann Hamer, BEd, AMBDA, DI(Cert)
Age range: 6-17. Boarders from 6-17
No. of pupils enrolled as at 1.1.92: 73
Junior: 26 Boys 4 Girls;
Senior: 30 Boys 13 Girls
Fees per annum: Day: £1150
Boarding: £2150

Type: Specialist Dyslexic and Asthma & Eczema

Religious denomination: Church of England

Member of: AWMVCISS

Curriculum: GCSE, RSA Examinations at 16+. Full curriculum, no withdrawal for specialist work. One hour timetabled each day on one-to-one. 30% Arts, 30% Sport, 30% General Education.

Entry requirements: Diagnosis of Dyslexia/need of specific learning difficulty structured teaching.

Normal curriculum schools with facilities to help pupils with Dyslexia or Special Learning Needs appear in Section Four.

John Catt Educational Limited
Great Glemham, Saxmundham,
Suffolk IP17 2DH
Tel: 0728 78666 Fax: 0728 78415

We specialise in consultancy, design and production of educational publications

Hawkhurst Court Dyslexia Centre

*Brighton College,
161 Eastern Road,
Brighton,
Sussex BN2 2AG
Tel: 0273 681484*

Head: Mrs M.F. Hollinshead, CertEd
(Member of British Dyslexia Association,
Association of Tutors)
Age range: 7-13+.
Boarders from 8
No. of pupils enrolled as at 1.1.92: 46
40 Boys; 6 Girls
Fees per annum:
Day: £5895
Weekly Boarding: £6990, Full Boarding: £7650

Type: Dyslexia School

Religious denomination: Church of England

Member of: Corporate member of British Dyslexia Association

Boys and girls, aged 7-13+ years are welcomed as day, full or weekly boarding pupils.

The Centre accepts children of average or above average intelligence with specific learning difficulties (Dyslexia), or pupils experiencing difficulty with language or numeracy, who are in need of specialist remedial teaching.

Considerable thought has been given to planning the curriculum, which includes English, Mathematics, Science, Geography, History, Scripture, Drama and Computer Studies. The superb facilities at Brighton College are used for Pottery, Games and Swimming, and the teaching of Science, Home Economics, Craft, Art and Music takes place in Brighton College Junior School. Hawkhurst Court pupils are fully integrated with members of the Junior School for Games and extra-curricular activities.

A new Boarding House has been opened for 20 boarders, close to the Centre. The resident Housemaster is responsible for the pastoral care of the boarders, and his wife, a qualified nurse, acts as Matron. The Housemaster is a specialist member of the teaching staff of the Centre.

The Helen Allison School

(Founded 1968)

*Longfield Road,
Meopham,
Kent DA13 0EW
Tel: 0474 814878 Fax: 0474 812033*

Head: Miss Lesley Marshall, AdvDipEd
Age range: 5-19. Boarders from 5
No. of pupils enrolled as at 1.1.92: 48
Junior: 26 Boys 4 Girls; Senior: 15 Boys 3 Girls
Fees per annum: Day: £18,585
Weekly Boarding: £27,648, Termly Boarding £33,555

Type: School for Children with Autism

Member of: The National Autistic Society

Curriculum: The School provides education for children aged 5 years to 19 years. The pupils will have to have a statement of educational needs following a modified National Curriculum with a direct teaching approach in a small group setting with a high staff ratio. The statement will include a medical diagnosis of autism or a psychologists report that the child presents with social and developmental problems which are in the autistic continuum.

Authoritative articles covering many important aspects of Special Learning Needs appear at the start of the Guide. Parents are urged to read them.

Kisimul School

(Founded 1977)

The Old Vicarage,
Swinderby,
Lincolnshire LN6 9LU
Tel: 052286 279

Head: Mr H.B. Matthews, BA, DipEd
Age range: 9-19. Boarders from 9
No. of pupils enrolled as at 1.1.92: 18
Junior: 4 Boys; Senior: 12 Boys 2 Girls
Fees per annum: Low £25,500; High £30,750

Type: Independent Residential School for children with severe or complex learning difficulties.

Approved by DES

Religious denomination: None

Curriculum: Children are assessed and taught on an individual basis. Initially programmes are based on a developmental curriculum (Communication, cognition, visual and auditory perception and motor, leading to Stages 1 and 2 of the National Curriculum). A wide range of group activities:- Music, Arts, Cookery, Woodwork, Swimming, Horse Riding, etc. also form part of the school day. In the Upper School, the programme includes Life Skills - Communication, Money Management, Travel and Home Skills, leading to independence. A high staff ratio is maintained throughout including a Speech Therapist. Extra-curricula activities include Cubs, Scouts, Gateway Clubs and Sunday School. No entry requirements.

Don't forget to make use of the Reader Enquiry Service cards at the back of the Guide if you want more information about the Schools or Colleges listed.

Linn Moor Residential School

(Founded 1975)

Peterculter, Aberdeen AB1 0PJ
Tel: 0224 732246

Head: Dr Robin Jackson
Age range: 6-18. Boarders from 6
No. of pupils enrolled as at 1.9.91: 30
Junior: 11 Boys 1 Girl; Senior: 11 Boys 7 Girls
Fees per annum: £21,946

Type: Residential Special School for pupils with severe learning difficulties and emotional and behavioural problems

Religious denomination: Non denominational

Member of: Scottish Independent Special Schools Group

Curriculum: Particular emphasis is placed on the development of a pupil's social and community living skills. Unique feature of the school is the wide range of therapeutic treatment provided - speech therapy, music therapy and dance therapy. Close professional working relationship between teaching and residential care staff in implementing pupils' individual programmes.

Entry requirements: Satisfactory completion of school's application form by the Local Authority Department (education and/or social work) proposing to sponsor the residential placement.

Academic and leisure facilities: Five modern

and well equipped classrooms: swimming pool, soft play area, adventure playground, BMX track, environmental studies trail. Opportunities for skiing, sailing, canoeing and hill walking in one of the most scenically attractive regions in Britain. High level of pupil participation in local youth organisations (eg, Cubs, Scouts, Brownies, Guides, etc.)

MacIntyre School

*The Old Manor House,
Wingrave,
Bucks HP22 4PD
Tel: 0296 681274 Fax: 0296 681091*

Head: Mrs J. Wadhams, CertEd, CSS
Age range: 5-19. Boarders from 5-19
No. of pupils enrolled as at 1.1.92: 41
Fees per annum:
£30,000-£35,000 (Under review)

Type: Residential School for children with mental disabilites - 52 week placement

Curriculum: Each child follows an individual programme of objectives. Language and communication are primary objectives, along with basic self-help skills, and the ability to make meaningful relationships with others. Core curriculum subjects are taught in creative ways which are meaningful to the children, complemented by speech, music, play and drama therapies, swimming and riding for the disabled. The staff draw on every affordable resource to stimulate, challenge and develop each child's potential in a happy caring environment.

MacIntyre is committed to integration into the community. We are involved in local social and leisure events including Scouts, Brownies and Gateway Club.

We specialise in consultancy, design, production and publication of:

- ☑ **Prospectuses**
- ☑ **Mini-prospectuses**
- ☑ **Newsletters**
- ☑ **Exhibition Materials**
- ☑ **Marketing**
- ☑ **Video Films**
- ☑ **School Magazines**
- ☑ **School Year Books**

Our experience and quality of craftsmanship enable us to give a service which we believe is unequalled by any other organisation at a highly competitive price.

For more details please telephone or write to:

John Catt Educational Limited
Great Glemham,
Saxmundham,
Suffolk IP17 2DH

Tel: 0728 78 666   Fax: 0728 78 415

Maple Hayes Dyslexia School

(Founded 1982)

*Maple Hayes Hall,
Abnalls Lane, Lichfield,
Staffs
Tel: 0543 264387*

Head: Dr E.N. Brown, PhD, MSc, BA, MINS, MSCME, AFBPS, CPsychol
Type: Approved by DES for dyslexic children
Age range: 7-16. Boarders from 7-16
No. of pupils enrolled as at 1.9.91: 107
Junior: 50 Boys Senior: 57 Boys
Fees per annum: Day: £2220
Boarding: £2770-£3120

Religious denomination: Inter-denominational

Member of: ISIS, ISIA, ISJC, ECIS

Curriculum: Normal curriculum (except French) to GCSE with specialist provision for dyslexic children without the degradation and unfortunate implications of withdrawal to a special unit.

Entry requirements: Psychologist's assessment of IQ and attainment, interview.

PROSPECTUSES
MINI-PROSPECTUSES
NEWSLETTERS
EXHIBITION MATERIALS
MARKETING
VIDEO FILMS
SCHOOL MAGAZINES
SCHOOL YEAR BOOKS

John Catt Educational Limited

Great Glemham
Saxmundham
Suffolk IP17 2DH

Tel 0728 78 666
Fax 0728 78 415

JOHN CATT EDUCATIONAL LIMITED

Mark College

(Founded 1986)

*Mark,
Highbridge,
Somerset TA9 4NP
Tel: 0278 64 632 Fax: 0278 64 426*

Head: Dr S. Chinn, BSc, PhD, DipEd.Man.
(Member of British Dyslexia Association (Chairman of International Conference Comm.))
Age range: 11-16. Boarders from 11-16
No. of pupils enrolled as at 1.1.92: 80
Fees per annum: Boarding: £9450

Type: DES Approved Secondary Boys School for Dyslexia/Sp.L.D.

Religious denomination: Church of England

Member of: ISAI, National Registration Scheme for Sp.l.d. Schools

Curriculum: Mark College offers a full curriculum to GCSE level with help in all subjects and extensive help in English and Mathematics. The College offers a good games programme and excellent care and social skill training.

Entry requirements: The majority of the College intake is at 11 years. Boys must be of average and above ability and have no primary behavioural problems.

Normal curriculum schools with facilities to help pupils with Dyslexia or Special Learning Needs appear in Section Four.

Nunnykirk Hall School

(Founded 1977)

*Netherwitton,
Morpeth,
Northumberland NE61 4PB
Tel: 0670 72685*

Head: Mr P.R.A. Booker, BA, CertEd, DipRemEd
Age range: 10-16. Boarders from 10-16
No. of pupils enrolled as at 1.1.92:
Up to 40 boarders and 10 day pupils
Fees per annum: On application

Type: Dept of Ed & Science approved special residential for Specific Learning Disabilities/Dyslexia, (Member of ISIS, (ISAI applied), Corporate Mbrs BDA)

Religious denomination: Interdenominational

Member of: ISIS, British Dyslexia Assn (Corp Mbrs), ISAI applied for

Curriculum: Full National Curriculum individually modified according to need or statement. Intensive structured remedial help by highly qualified staff. GCSE in up to 10 subjects. Wide variety of extra curricular activities including Duke of Edinburgh Awards. The homely and supportive residential setting provides a 'whole child' approach.

Entry requirements: By interview and psychologist's report.

Authoritative articles covering many important aspects of Special Learning Needs appear at the start of the Guide. Parents are urged to read them.

The Old Rectory School

*Brettenham,
Ipswich,
Suffolk IP7 7QR
Tel: (0449) 736404 Fax: (0449) 737881*

Patron: Sir Michael Weston KCMG CVO
British Ambassador to Kuwait
Head: M.A.Phillips, LTh, DipEd, CertEdPsych
Educational Pyschologist: Dr H.T.Chasty, MSc, PhD, ABPsS
Adviser in Specialist Teaching: Dr Beve Hornsby, MSc, MEd, PhD, ABPsS
Adviser for LEA: Michael Burnham
Age range: 7 - 13
No. of pupils enrolled as at 1.9.91:
Boys 35 Girls 6; No. of boarders: 36
Fees: on application

Type: Co-educational Special Dyslexia School

THE OLD RECTORY IS A SPECIALIST SCHOOL FOR CHILDREN who are suffering from Specific Learning Difficulties - commonly called DYSLEXIA.

The School is accredited by the National Registration Council (SENIC) and is a Corporate Member of the BRITISH DYSLEXIA ASSOCIATION.

The aim of the Old Rectory is to help children realise their true potential within a family environment. In their past schooling they may well have been misunderstood and their problems blamed on laziness or stupidity. Constant failure may well have resulted in the child suffering from a severe lack of confidence which will only be corrected in a sympathetic and understanding environment. It is for this reason that the Old Rectory has been established. Children enjoy the comfort, security and care of a family atmosphere as well as receiving specialist and individual remedial help.

Although the emphasis is on the acquisition of literacy and numeracy skills, all children follow the National Curriculum.

Depending on the severity of their difficulties

and on their progress, children remain at the Old Rectory for a *minimum of one year and a maximum of two years*. The Headmaster believes that it is his mutual responsibility with parents, to find suitable placement in other schools when children leave.

The Old Rectory is set in five acres of landscaped grounds at the edge of a peaceful Suffolk village adjacent to the church and enjoys uninterrupted country views in all directions.

As well as a full range of extra curricular activities the school enjoys links with an IAPS boarding school, set in 80 acres and situated approximately one mile away. The children are able to make use of its swimming pool, tennis courts and playing fields.

Parayhouse School

(Founded 1964)

*St John's, World's End,
Kings Road,
Chelsea,
London SW10 0LU
Tel: 071 352 2882*

Head: Mrs S.L. Jackson, CertEd, DipEd
(Complex Learning Handicap)
Age range: 4-18
No. of pupils enrolled as at 1.1.92:
Junior: 16 Boys 14 Girls; Senior: 7 Boys 16 Girls
Fees per annum: £5850 - £6450

Type: Specialist Learning Difficulties

Religious denomination: None

Member of: ISAI

Curriculum: Parayhouse School was established in 1964, changing in 1983 to provide exclusively for children with a wide range of Learning Difficulties, from 4 to 18 years of age.

All children follow an individual programme within a structured class framework, and all have full access to the National Curriculum Core and Foundation subjects. Qualified, experienced teachers are supported by a Speech Therapist, Science and Computer teacher, Physiotherapist, specialist teachers of Art, Design, Music, Singing and Classroom Assistants.

Entry to the School is by Assessment during a day in School. Early application is advised and an informative Prospectus is available on request.

We specialise in consultancy, design, production and publication of:

- [✓] **Prospectuses**
- [✓] **Mini-prospectuses**
- [✓] **Newsletters**
- [✓] **Exhibition Materials**
- [✓] **Marketing**
- [✓] **Video Films**
- [✓] **School Magazines**
- [✓] **School Year Books**

Our experience and quality of craftsmanship enable us to give a service which we believe is unequalled by any other organisation at a highly competitive price.

John Catt Educational Limited
Great Glemham,
Saxmundham,
Suffolk IP17 2DH
Tel: 0728 78 666 Fax: 0728 78 415

Don't forget to make use of the Reader Enquiry Service cards at the back of the Guide if you want more information about the Schools or Colleges listed.

St Josephs School

(Founded 1915)

*Amlets Lane,
Cranleigh, Surrey GU6 7NQ
Tel: 0483 272449*

Principal: Mr A. Lowry
Age range: 5-19. Boarders from 5-19
No. of pupils enrolled as at 1.1.92:
Junior: 13 Boys 1 Girl; Senior: 25 Boys 3 Girls
Sixth Form: 22 Boys 6 Girls
Fees per annum:
Day: £11,000; Boarding: £16,500

Type: Moderate/severe/specific LD. Speech and language impairment.

Religious denomination: Roman Catholic RC Diocese of Arundel and Brighton

Curriculum: Pupils between 5 and 16 have access to the complete range of National Curriculum subjects as well as PSE, Careers, Health Education and RE. Teaching staff aim to differentiate the curriculum to pupils with learning difficulties with special emphasis placed on pupils with speech and language impairment. Students in the 16 to 19 age range follow a curriculum containing an entitlement to core, vocational and occupational studies with special emphasis placed on the development of independence-related skills. A team of speech therapists provides support on both a withdrawal and 'in-class' basis. Moreover, St Josephs believes in providing a 24 hour curriculum whereby residential and teaching staff are fully informed and involved in activities across the broad spectrum of the school day. School staff are closely involved with the local authority (Surrey CC), having access to the full range of its staff development programme and as full members of its TVEI Extension.

Entry requirements: Initial contact may be made by parents, LEA or careers service leading to a school based assessment period.

Examinations offered: Pupils and students have the opportunity to undertake examination courses where appropriate including pre-GCSE Certificate in Maths, BTec and NVQ. The school also operates a Record of Achievement programme over the complete age range.

Where it is considered beneficial, some pupils and students attend local mainstream schools and colleges.

Academic and leisure facilities: Pupils from 5 to 16 attend a purpose built school block which is both well resourced and equipped. Students from 16 to 19 attend a separate suite of modern rooms designed to encourage a more mature working atmosphere. Residential accommodation for the 5 to 16 pupils is in the main building while the 16 to 19 students and staff stay in self-contained houses situated both on and off the campus. Other facilities include a swimming pool, gymnasium, art room, pottery, outdoor children's play area, indoor soft play area, tennis court, and extensive grounds with sports fields, landscaped features, wooded areas and small wildlife ponds.

Religious activities: RE is taught as part of the school curriculum and attempts to provide a broadly Christian teaching as well as an insight into other faiths and is fully supported by the Diocese. The campus also has a modern Chapel which is used to hold services on Sundays and Holy days to which all pupils, students and staff are invited.

Sheiling School
Camphill Community

(Founded 1952)

*Park Road,
Thornbury,
Bristol BS12 1HP
Tel: 0454 412194*

Head: The Chairman of the College of Teachers
Age range: 6-16. Boarders from 6-16
No. of pupils enrolled as at 1.1.92: 53
27 Boys 26 Girls
Fees per annum: £11,949

Type: Independent Boarding, wide variety of learning difficulties and behaviour problems.

Religious denomination: Christian non-denominational

Member of: Association of Camphill Communities

Curriculum: The Curative Education offered at this Camphill School Community is founded on the teachings of Rudolf Steiner - the Waldorf curriculum is adapted to the needs of the children in classes of 10-15 children of their own age group. In the homely atmosphere of the six residential houses on the beautiful school estate the children acquire social awareness and social skills. Therapeutic activities to help a child overcome specific problems which interfere with educational and social development are offered in the classroom and in the house in which the child lives. More specialised treatments are given by therapists in separate sessions.

Entry requirements: Interview with the Medical Officer and appropriate staff.

Directory of Schools specialising in Emotional/Behavioural Difficulties

Avon

HIGHDENE SCHOOL
The Laurels, Cribbs Causeway,
Avon BS10 7TU
Tel: (0272) 501857
Head: T Bridgeman
Type: Boys Boarding 13-18
No of pupils: 14 No of boarders 14
Special Needs: EBD MLD
Approved Independent

WARLEIGH SCHOOL
Warleigh Manor, Bathford, Bath, Avon BA1 8EE
Tel: (0225) 858154
Head: L Alderman
Type: Boys Boarding 7-16
No of pupils: 18 No of boarders 18
Special Needs: EBD
Approved Independent

Cheshire

CHAIGELEY SCHOOL
Thelwall, Warrington, Cheshire WA4 2TE
Tel: (0925) 752357
Head: P W Duffy
Type: Boys Boarding 10-16
No of pupils: 48 No of boarders 48
Special Needs: EBD MLD
Non - maintained

Cornwall

WHITSTONE HEAD SCHOOL
Whitstone, Holsworthy, Cornwall EX22 6TJ
Tel: (0288) 84251
Head: E Gent
Type: Co-educational Boarding & Day 10-17
No of pupils: B32 G8 No of boarders 40
Special Needs: DYS EBD MLD
Approved Independent

Cumbria

EDEN GROVE SCHOOL
Bolton, Appleby, Cumbria CA16 6AJ
Tel: (07683) 61346
Head: B E Cole
Type: Boys Boarding 8-16
No of pupils: 64 No of boarders 64
Special Needs: EBD MLD
Approved Independent

GREYSTONE HOUSE SCHOOL
Great Strickland, Penrith, Cumbria CA10 3DJ
Tel: (09312) 300
Head: B M J McCarthy
Type: Boys Boarding 11-16
No of pupils: 19 No of boarders 19
Special Needs: EBD
Approved Independent

RIVERSIDE SCHOOL
Whassett, Milnthorpe, Cumbria LA7 7DN
Tel: (05375) 62006
Head: G H Leake
Type: Co-educational Boarding & Day 9-17
No of pupils: B36 G36 No of boarders 72
Special Needs: EBD MLD SpL
Approved Independent

WITHERSLACK HALL
Grange-over-Sands, Witherslack, Cumbria LA11 6SD
Tel: (044852) 397/419
Heads: Mr & Mrs J Horner
Type: Boys Boarding 11-16
No of pupils: 66 No of boarders 66
Special Needs: DYS EBD SpL
Approved Independent

Derbyshire

ROWEN HOUSE SCHOOL
50 Holbrook Road, Belper, Derbyshire DE5 1PB
Tel: (0773) 827632
Heads: Mr & Mrs B Purdy & Neil Redfern
Type: Girls Boarding & Day 11-18
No of pupils: 15
Special Needs: EBD
Approved Independent

Devon

CHELFHAM MILL SCHOOL
Chelfham, Barnstaple, Devon EX32 7LA
Tel: (0271) 850448
Head: Dr J R Burlam
Type: Boys Boarding & Day 6-12
No of pupils: 51 No of boarders 46
Special Needs: EBD MLD
Approved Independent

CHELFHAM SENIOR SCHOOL
Bere Alston, Yelverston, Devon PL20 7EX
Tel: (0822) 840379
Head: R P Mendham
Type: Boys Boarding & Day 11-17
No of pupils: 38 No of boarders 36
Special Needs: DYS EBD MLD SpL
Approved Independent

Emotional/Behavioural Difficulties

KILWORTHY HOUSE
Trelawny Road, Tavistock,
Devon PL19 OJN
Tel: (0822) 612610
Head: K M Coutson
Type: Co-educational Boarding 12-18
No of pupils: B8 G8 No of boarders 16
Special Needs: EBD MLD
Approved Independent

MARLAND SCHOOL
Petersmarland, Torrington,
Devon EX3 8QQ
Tel: (08055) 324
Head: W K Gerrish
Type: Boys Boarding 11-16
No of pupils: 40 No of boarders 40
Special Needs: EBD MLD SpL
Approved Independent

NETHERTON HALL SCHOOL
Farway, Colyton, Devon EX13 6EB
Tel: (040487) 261
Head: E F Barrett
Type: Co-educational Boarding 10-17
No of pupils: B42 G7 No of boarders 49
Special Needs: EBD MLD
Approved Independent

ST LUKE'S 16 PLUS FOR INDEPENDENT TRAINING
Fair Oaks, Dawlish Road, Teignmouth,
Devon TQ14 8TG
Tel: (0626) 777171
Head: J D Brandwood
Type: Co-educational Boarding 16-0
No of pupils: 20 No of boarders 20
Special Needs: EBD MLD SLD
Approved Independent

ST LUKE'S SCHOOL
Exeter Road, Teignmouth,
Devon TQ14 9JG
Tel: (0626) 778328
Head: J D Brandwood
Type: Boys Boarding 11-17
No of pupils: 20 No of boarders 20
Special Needs: EBD MLD
Approved Independent

ST THOMAS MORE'S SCHOOL
East Allington, Totnes,
Devon TQ9 7QF
Tel: (054852) 273
Head: D R Eglin
Type: Boys Boarding 9-16
No of pupils: 70 No of boarders 70
Special Needs: EBD MLD SpL
Approved Independent

Dorset

GRANGEWOOD HALL SCHOOL
24 St John's Hill, Wimborne, Dorset BH21 1BZ
Tel: (0202) 883954
Head: M & S E Jee & S R Phillips
Type: Co-educational Boarding 6-12
No of pupils: B24 G8 No of boarders 32
Special Needs: EBD MLD
Approved Independent

ST FRANCIS SCHOOL
Hooke, Beaminster, Dorset DT8 3NY
Tel: (0308) 862260
Head: P R Barry
Type: Boys Boarding & Day 10-17
No of pupils: 45 No of boarders 45
Special Needs: EBD
Non - maintained

Essex

CHELMER RESIDENTIAL SCHOOL
Maldon Road, Chelmsford, Essex CM2 7RZ
Tel: (0245) 72200
Head: C J Wright
Type: Boys Boarding 12-16
No of pupils: 42 No of boarders 42
Special Needs: EBD MLD SpL
Approved Independent

EDWARDSTONE HOUSE SCHOOL
Sherbourne Street, Edwardstone, Boxford, Colchester,
Essex CO6 5PD
Tel: (0787) 210272
Head: C J Wright
Type: Boys Boarding 9-13
No of pupils: 15 No of boarders 15
Special Needs: EBD MLD SpL
Approved Independent

GREENWOOD SCHOOL
25 Mill Chase, Halstead, Essex CO9 2DQ
Tel: (0787) 472002
Head: D Makey
Type: Girls Boarding 7-17
No of pupils: 70 No of boarders 70
Special Needs: DYS EBD MLD SpL
Non - maintained

OXLEY PARKER SCHOOL
Mill Road, Colchester, Essex CO4 5JF
Tel: (0206) 853222
Head: D P King
Type: Boys Boarding 7-17
No of pupils: 80 No of boarders 80
Special Needs: DYS EBD MLD SpL
Non - maintained

Gloucestershire

ADLESTROP PARK SCHOOL
Moreton-in-Marsh, Gloucestershire
Tel: (0608) 658 253
Head: A John-Pritchard
Type: Boys Boarding 11-16
Special Needs: EBD
Approved Independent

BADGEWORTH COURT SCHOOL
Badgeworth, Cheltenham, Gloucestershire GL51 5UL
Tel: (0452) 712439
Head: A J B Hurley
Type: Boys Boarding & Day 10-17
No of pupils: 72
Special Needs: EBD
Independent

NEW BARNS SCHOOL
Church Lane, Toddington, Cheltenham,
Gloucestershire GL54 5DQ
Tel: (0242) 621200
Head: R Alston
Type: Co-educational Boarding 8-14
No of pupils: B18 G10 No of boarders 28
Special Needs: EBD
Approved Independent

BERROW WOOD SCHOOL
Pendock, Gloucester, GL19 3PR
Tel: (068481) 225
Head: A Gorton
Type: Boys Boarding 10-11
No of pupils: 43 No of boarders 43
Special Needs: DYS EBD MLD PHe SLD
Approved Independent

COTSWOLD CHINE HOME SCHOOL
Box, Stroud, Gloucestershire GL6 9AG
Tel: (0453) 832398
Head: C Troy
Type: Co-educational Boarding 10-16
No of pupils: B26 G9 No of boarders 35
Special Needs: EBD MLD SpL
Approved Independent

SALESIAN SCHOOL
Blaisdon Hall, Longhope, Gloucestershire GL17 0AQ
Tel: (0452) 830247
Head: Father P Kenna
Type: Boys Boarding 10-16
No of pupils: 30 No of boarders 30
Special Needs: EBD MLD
Approved Independent

Hampshire

ALLINGTON MANOR SCHOOL
Allington Lane, Fair Oak,
Hampshire S05 7DE
Tel: (0703) 692621
Head: Dr L F Lowenstein
Type: Co-educational Boarding & Day 8-16
No of pupils: B13 G12 No of boarders 25
Special Needs: DYS EBD MH MLD PH PHe SpD SpL VIS
Non - maintained

COXLEASE SCHOOL
High Coxlease House, Clay Hill, Lyndhurst,
Hampshire SO43 7DE
Tel: (0703) 283633
Type: Boys Boarding 9-17
No of pupils: 49 No of boarders 49
Special Needs: EBD MLD
Approved Independent

FREEFOLK HOUSE
Laverstoke, Whitchurch, Hampshire RG28 7PB
Tel: (0256) 892634
Head: R Huggett
Type: Co-educational Boarding & Day 14-19
No of pupils: 20 No of boarders 20
Special Needs: DYS EBD SpL
Independent

GRATELEY HOUSE SCHOOL
Grateley, Andover, Hampshire SP11 8JR
Tel: (0264) 889751
Head: N J Saltrese
Type: Co-educational Boarding 11-16
No of pupils: B14 G28 No of boarders 42
Special Needs: EBD MLD
Approved Independent

HILL HOUSE SCHOOL
Rope Hill, Boldre, Lymington,
Hampshire SO41 8NE
Tel: (0590) 672147
Head: A Summer
Type: Boys Boarding 7-13
No of pupils: 40 No of boarders 40
Special Needs: EBD MLD
Approved Independent

THE LODDON SCHOOL
Sherfield-on-Loddon, Basingstoke, Hampshire RG27 OJD
Tel: (0256) 882394
Head: Miss M Cornick
Type: Co-educational Boarding 7-19
No of pupils: 20 No of boarders 20
Special Needs: AUT BI EBD MH SLD SpD VIS

ST EDWARDS SCHOOL
Melchet Court, Sherfield English, Romsey, Hampshire S051 6ZR
Tel: (0794) 884271
Head: D J Doyle
Type: Boys Boarding 10-16
No of pupils: 90 No of boarders 90
Special Needs: EBD MLD SpL
Approved Independent

SOUTHLANDS SCHOOL
Vicar's Hill, Boldre, Lymington, Hampshire S041 8QB
Tel: (0590) 675350
Head: J D Jerwood
Type: Boys Boarding 11-17
No of pupils: 72 No of boarders 72
Special Needs: EBD
Approved Independent

Hertfordshire

THE HOUSE IN THE SUN SCHOOL
Hengrove, nr Tring, Hertfordshire HP23 6LE
Tel: (0296) 622136
Head: A F Gobell
Type: Girls Boarding 10-17
No of pupils: 24 No of boarders 24
Special Needs: EBD MLD
Approved Independent

SOUTH LODGE SCHOOL
High Street, Baldock, Hertfordshire SG7 6BX
Tel: (0462) 892715
Head: Mrs R Kirkwood
Type: Girls Boarding 12-18
No of pupils: 26 No of boarders 26
Special Needs: EBD MLD
Approved Independent

Kent

CALDECOTT COMMUNITY SCHOOL
Ashford, Kent TN25 5NH
Tel: (0233) 623954
Head: M R Jinks
Type: Co-educational Boarding & Day 4-16
No of pupils: B36 G18 No of boarders 52
Special Needs: EBD MLD SpL
Non - maintained

PORT REGIS SCHOOL
Kingsgate, Broadstairs, Kent CT10 3PT
Tel: (0843) 62561
Head: Sister S Cronin
Type: Co-educational Boarding 5-13
No of pupils: B18 G6 No of boarders 24
Special Needs: EBD MLD
Non - maintained

RED HILL SCHOOL
Charlton Court, East Sutton, Maidstone,
Kent ME17 3DQ
Tel: (0622) 843104
Head: A J Rimmer
Type: Boys Boarding 11-17
No of pupils: 35 No of boarders 35
Special Needs: EBD
Non - maintained

RIPPLEVALE SCHOOL
Deal, Kent CT14 8JG
Tel: (0304) 373866
Head: A McCarthy
Type: Boys Boarding 9-17
No of pupils: 43 No of boarders 43
Special Needs: EBD MLD SpL
Approved Independent

Lancashire

BEECH TREE SCHOOL
Meadow Lane, Bamber Bridge, Preston,
Lancashire PR5 8LN
Tel: (0772) 213131
Head: Miss N M Story
Type: Co-educational Boarding 7-14
No of pupils: B13 G4 No of boarders 17
Special Needs: Bl D EBD MH MLD PH PHe SLD
SMH SpD VIS
Approved Independent

CEDAR HOUSE SCHOOL
Kirby Lonsdale, Carnforth, Lancashire LA6 2HW
Tel: (0524) 271181
Head: G S McEwan
Type: Co-educational Boarding 10-16
No of pupils: 56 No of boarders 56
Special Needs: EBD
Approved Independent

NUGENT HOUSE SCHOOL
Carr Mill Road, Billinge, Wigan,
Lancashire WN5 7TT
Tel: (0744) 892551
Head: C G Mills
Type: Boys Boarding & Day 8-17
No of pupils: 75
Special Needs: EBD MLD SpL
Approved Independent

UNDERLEY GARDEN SCHOOL
Kirby Lonsdale, Via Carnforth, Lancashire LA6 2DZ
Tel: (05242) 71569
Head: Mr & Mrs D W Cooper
Type: Co-educational Boarding 8-16
No of pupils: B21 G21 No of boarders 42
Special Needs: DYS EBD SpL
Approved Independent

UNDERLEY HALL SCHOOL
Kirby Lonsdale, Via Carnforth,
Lancashire LA6 2HE
Tel: (05242) 71206
Head: Mr & Mrs D W Cooper
Type: Boys Boarding 9-16
No of pupils: 84 No of boarders 84
Special Needs: DYS EBD SpL
Approved Independent

Leicestershire

THE GRANGE SCHOOL
Knossington, Oakham, Leicestershire LE15 8LY
Tel: (066477) 264
Head: Dr A J Smith
Type: Boys Boarding 7-17
No of pupils: 60 No of boarders 60
Special Needs: EBD
Approved Independent

Lincolnshire

BROUGHTON HOUSE SCHOOL
High Street, Brant Broughton, Lincoln LN5 OSL
Tel: (0400) 72929
Head: A D Lemon
Type: Boys Boarding 11-16
No of pupils: 41 No of boarders 41
Special Needs: EBD MLD
Approved Independent

London

THE LEARNING CENTRE
89 Parkway, London NW1 7PP
Tel: (081) 348 1428
Head: Mrs N Janis-Norton
Type: Co-educational Boarding & Day 4-18
Special Needs: EBD SpL

Merseyside

CLARENCE HOUSE SCHOOL
West Lane, Freshfield, Merseyside L37 7AS
Tel: (07048) 72151
Head: A Esmat
Type: Co-educational Boarding & Day 10-16
No of pupils: B75 G25 No of boarders 60
Special Needs: EBD
Approved Independent

WEST KIRBY RESIDENTIAL SCHOOL
Meols Drive, West Kirby, Wirral, Merseyside L48 5DH
Tel: (051) 632 3201
Head: T I F Price
Type: Co-educational Boarding & Day 9-16
No of pupils: B55 G40 No of boarders 60
Special Needs: EBD MLD PH PHe SpD SpL VIS
Non - maintained

Norfolk

HILBRE SCHOOL
Holway Road, Sheringham, Norfolk NR26 8NP
Tel: (0263) 822800
Head: D C Younger
Type: Co-educational Boarding 6-12
No of pupils: B21 G3 No of boarders 24
Special Needs: EBD MLD
Approved Independent

SHERIDAN HOUSE SCHOOL & FAMILY THERAPY UNIT
Southburgh, Thetford, Norfolk IP25 7TJ
Tel: (0953) 850494
Head: F R G G Tyler
Type: Co-educational Boarding & Day 10-16
No of pupils: B6 G4 No of boarders 12
Special Needs: EBD
Approved Independent

Northamptonshire

POTTERSPURY LODGE SCHOOL
Potterspury, Towcester, Northamptonshire NN12 7LL
Tel: (0908) 542912
Head: Miss G Lietz
Type: Boys Boarding 8-16   *No of pupils:* 45 No of boarders 45
Special Needs: AUT EBD MLD SpD SpL
Approved Independent

Oxfordshire

BESSELS LEIGH SCHOOL
Besselsleigh, Abingdon, Oxfordshire OX13 5QB
Tel: (0865) 390436
Head: F A Caulfield
Type: Boys Boarding 11-16
Special Needs: EBD
Non - maintained

MULBERRY BUSH SCHOOL
Standlake, Witney, Oxfordshire OX8 7RW
Tel: (0865) 300202
Head: R Rollinson
Type: Co-educational Boarding 6-11
No of pupils: 36 No of boarders 36
Special Needs: EBD
Non - maintained

Shropshire

COTSBROOK COMMUNITY
Higford, Shifnal, Shropshire TF11 9ET
Tel: (0952) 87237
Head: M Melaniphy
Type: Co-educational Boarding 11-16
No of pupils: B15 G15 No of boarders 30
Special Needs: EBD
Approved Independent

CRUCKTON HALL
Cruckton, Shrewsbury, Shropshire SY5 8PR
Tel: (0743) 860009
Head: I D Barrett
Type: Boys Boarding 8-16
No of pupils: 42 No of boarders 42
Special Needs: EBD
Approved Independent

HILLTOP SCHOOL & THERAPEUTIC COMMUNITY
Fishmore Road, Ludlow, Shropshire SY8 3DP
Tel: (0588) 672071
Head: N Wainwright
Type: Co-educational Boarding 11-16
No of pupils: B17 G8 No of boarders 25
Special Needs: EBD MLD
Approved Independent

SHOTTON HALL SCHOOL
Harmer Hill, Shrewsbury, Shropshire SY4 3DW
Tel: (0939) 290376
Head: J W Parker
Type: Boys Boarding 10-18
No of pupils: 35 No of boarders 35
Special Needs: EBD MLD
Approved Independent

Somerset

CHILDSCOURT SCHOOL
Lattiford House, Wincanton, Somerset BA9 8AH
Tel: (0963) 32213
Heads: Miss J P J Malcolm & Mrs M H Wilkins
Type: Co-educational Boarding 9-16
No of pupils: B20 G25 No of boarders 45
Special Needs: EBD EPI SpD VIS
Approved Independent

THE MARCHANT-HOLLIDAY SCHOOL
North Cheriton, Templecombe, Somerset BA8 0AH
Tel: (0963) 33234
Head: J M Robertson
Type: Boys Boarding 6-13
No of pupils: 37 No of boarders 37
Special Needs: DYS EBD SpL
Approved Independent

Suffolk

BRAMFIELD HOUSE
Walpole Road, Bramfield, Halesworth,
Suffolk IP19 9AB
Tel: (0986) 84235
Head: M G Read
Type: Boys Boarding & Day 10-16
No of pupils: 35 No of boarders 35
Special Needs: EBD MLD
Approved Independent

KESGRAVE HALL SCHOOL
Kesgrave, Ipswich, Suffolk IP5 7PU
Tel: (0473) 624755
Head: M G Smith
Type: Boys Boarding 11-18
No of pupils: 50 No of boarders 50
Special Needs: DYS EBD SpL
Approved Independent

THE RYES SCHOOL
Little Henny, Sudbury, Suffolk CO10 7EA
Tel: (0787) 74998
Head: Mrs R Stamp
Type: Co-educational Boarding & Day 7-16
No of pupils: B15 G13 No of boarders 27
Special Needs: EBD MLD SpL
Approved Independent

East Sussex

THE CHALVINGTON TRUST SCHOOL
Firle Road, Seaford, East Sussex BN25 3JE
Tel: (0323) 892676
Head: M Whinney & P Estell
Type: Co-educational Boarding 11-16
Special Needs: EBD
Approved Independent

THE MOUNT CAMPHILL STEINER SCHOOL
Wadhurst, East Sussex TN5 6PT
Tel: (0892) 882025
Type: Co-educational Boarding 14-25
No of pupils: B22 G20 No of boarders 42
Special Needs: EBD MH MLD
Approved Independent

ST VINCENT'S SCHOOL
80 St Saviours Road, St Leonards-on-Sea,
East Sussex TN38 0AT
Tel: (0424) 439210
Head: Mrs V Peters
Type: Girls Boarding & Day 10-19
No of pupils: 50 No of boarders 45
Special Needs: DYS EBD PHe SpD SpL
Non - maintained

SPINNEY SCHOOL
Little London, Heathfield, East Sussex TN21 0NU
Tel: (0435) 866304
Head: T P O'Hare
Type: Boys Boarding & Day 10-17
No of pupils: 34 No of boarders 34
Special Needs: EBD MLD SpL
Approved Independent

STONECOURT SCHOOL
Gillsmans Hill, St Leonards-on-Sea, East Sussex
Tel: (0424) 430277
Head: J P Crawley
Type: Girls Boarding 11+
No of pupils: 24 No of boarders 24
Special Needs: EBD MLD

West Sussex

DEDISHAM SCHOOL
Slinfold, Horsham, West Sussex RH13 7RA
Tel: (0403) 790257
Head: G C Pickering
Type: Co-educational Boarding 8-16+
No of pupils: B28 G7 No of boarders 35
Special Needs: AUT DYS EBD MH MLD SLD SMH SpD SpL
Approved Independent

FARNEY CLOSE SCHOOL
Bolney Court, Bolney, Haywards Heath,
West Sussex RH17 5RD
Tel: (0444) 881811
Head: J R Thompson
Type: Co-educational Boarding 8-17
No of pupils: B50 G25 No of boarders 75
Special Needs: EBD
Approved Independent

MUNTHAN HOUSE SCHOOL
Barns Green, Horsham, West Sussex RH13 7NJ
Tel: (0403) 730302
Head: A G Train
Type: Boys Boarding 7-18
No of pupils: 50 No of Boarders 50
Special Needs: DYS EBD MLD
Non - maintained

PHILPOTS MANOR SCHOOL
West Hoathly, East Grinstead, West Sussex RH19 4PR
Tel: (0342) 810268
Head: Mrs S A Merrifield
Type: Co-educational Boarding 6-18
No of pupils: B43 G22 No of boarders 65
Special Needs: DYS EBD MLD PHe
Approved Independent

Tyne and Wear

FEVERSHAM SCHOOL
Hexham Road, Walbottle, Tyne and Wear NE15 8HW
Tel: (091) 229 0111
Head: D Wilson
Type: Co-educational Boarding 8-19
No of pupils: B54 G10 No of boarders 64
Special Needs: EBD MLD SpL
Non - maintained

Wiltshire

SUTCLIFFE SCHOOL
Winsley House, Winsley, Bradford-on-Avon,
Wiltshire BA15 2LE
Tel: (0225) 722144
Head: P E Jones
Type: Boys Boarding 9-16
Special Needs: EBD
Non - maintained

North Yorkshire

BRECKENBROUGH SCHOOL
Thirsk, North Yorkshire YO7 4EN
Tel: (0845) 587238
Head: P E Jackson
Type: Boys Boarding & Day 9-17
No of pupils: 48 No of boarders 47
Special Needs: EBD
Non - maintained

SPRING HILL SCHOOL
Palace Road, Ripon,
North Yorkshire HG4 3HN
Tel: (0765) 603320
Head: D K Searle
Type: Co-educational 10-17
Special Needs: EBD MLD SLD
Approved Independent

South Yorkshire

HESLEY HALL SCHOOL
Tickhill, Doncaster, South Yorkshire DN11 9HH
Tel: (0302) 868313
Head: M Gray
Type: Boys Boarding 7-13
No of pupils: 63 No of boarders 63
Special Needs: EBD MLD
Approved Independent

WILSIC HALL SCHOOL
Wadworth, Doncaster, South Yorkshire DN11 9AG
Tel: (0302) 856382
Head: N R Linsley
Type: Boys Boarding 13-16
No of pupils: 66 No of boarders 66
Special Needs: EBD
Approved Independent

West Yorkshire

HILTON GRANGE SCHOOL
Bramhope, Leeds, West Yorkshire LS16 9HU
Tel: (0532) 842127
Head: D J Freeman
Type: Co-educational Boarding & Day 8-18
Special Needs: EBD MLD
Non - maintained

WILLIAM HENRY SMITH SCHOOL
Boothroyd, Brighouse, West Yorkshire HD6 3JW
Tel: (0484) 710123
Head: R P Crampton
Type: Boys Boarding 11-19
Special Needs: EBD
Approved Independent

SCOTLAND

Angus

PARKVIEW SCHOOL
309 Blackness Road, Dundee, Angus DD2 1SH
Tel: (0382) 67903
Head: Mr & Mrs J B Scanlin
Type: Co-educational
Special Needs: EBD MLD
Independent

Ayrshire

RED BRAE RESIDENTIAL SCHOOL
24 Alloway Road, Maybole, Ayrshire KA19 8AA
Tel: (0655) 83104
Head: R J F Dalrymple
Type: Boys Boarding 8-16
Special Needs: EBD

Fife

HOUSE OF FALKLAND SCHOOL
Falkland, Fife KY7 7AE
Tel: (0337) 57268
Head: T Swan
Type: Boys Boarding 11-16
No of pupils: 42 No of boarders 42
Special Needs: EBD
Approved Independent

Midlothian

HARMENY SCHOOL
Balerno, Midlothian EH14 7JY
Tel: (031) 449 3938
Head: D Pfluger
Type: Co-educational Boarding 6-12
Special Needs: EBD SpL

Perthshire

OCHIL TOWER (RUDOLF STEINER) SCHOOL
Auchterarder, Perthshire PH3 1AD
Tel: (0764) 62416
Head: J M Surkamp
Type: Co-educational Boarding & Day 6-18
No of pupils: B16 G12 No of boarders 28
Special Needs: DYS EBD MH MLD PH SLD SMH SpD SpL
Approved Independent

Wigtownshire

MERTON HALL
Newton Stewart, Wigtownshire DG8 6QL
Tel: (0671) 2447
Head: P B & E E Richards
Type: Co-educational Boarding & Day 7-16
No of pupils: B17 G6 No of boarders 20
Special Needs: EBD
Approved Independent

WOODLANDS SCHOOL
Corsbie Road, Newton Stewart, Wigtownshire DG8 6JB
Tel: (0671) 2480/3740
Head: P K Machell
Type: Co-educational Boarding 10-17
No of pupils: B34 G8 No of boarders 42
Special Needs: EBD MLD SpL VIS

Display Listings of Schools specialising in Emotional/Behavioural Difficulties

Beech Tree School

(Founded 1985)

*Meadow Lane,
Bamber Bridge, Nr Preston,
Lancashire PR5 8LN
Tel: 0772 323131 Fax: 0772 322187*

Head: Nina M. Story, MEd
Age range: Boarders from 7-14 at entry
No. of pupils enrolled as at 1.1.92: 17
11 Boys 6 Girls
Fees per annum: Boarding: £54,600

Type: Residential School catering for children with severe learning difficulties and challenging behaviour.

Curriculum: To provide consistent short term, remedial, residential education for children with severe learning difficulties who have developed challenging behaviour. The placement is for two years with an initial three month trial period.

Entry requirements: None.

We specialise in consultancy, design, production and publication of:

☑ **Prospectuses**

☑ **Mini-prospectuses**

☑ **Newsletters**

☑ **Exhibition Materials**

☑ **Marketing**

☑ **Video Films**

☑ **School Magazines**

☑ **School Year Books**

Our experience and quality of craftsmanship enable us to give a service which we believe is unequalled by any other organisation at a highly competitive price.

John Catt Educational Limited
Great Glemham,
Saxmundham,
Suffolk IP17 2DH
Tel: 0728 78 666   Fax: 0728 78 415

Downshead School

(Founded 1984)

*Southdown Road,
Seaford,
East Sussex BN25 4JS
Tel: 0323 895214*

Heads: Miss M Desmond, Mr R J Blackman, RGN, MND
Age range: 9-16. Boarders from 9-16
No. of pupils enrolled as at 1.1.92: 10
Junior: Boys 5 Girls 1
Senior: Boys 2 Girls 1
Sixth form: Boys 1
Range of fees per annum (incl VAT) as at 1.1.92:
Boarding: £29,022.50-£30,244.50

Type: Registered school, awaiting approval. Needs catered for: emotional, behavioural, social, educational.

Religious affiliation: Multi-lateral

Member of: SCA

Curriculum: English, Cambridge Mathematics and Science, History, Geography, Religious Education, Design and Technology (including car mechanics), Sport, Music, Animal Husbandry, Health Education.

Entry requirements: Entry after full assessment and initial visit or introduction at present placement, home, *etc.*

A full range of guides to UK Schools is also published by John Catt Educational.

Normal curriculum schools with facilities to help pupils with Dyslexia or Special Learning Needs appear in Section Four.

Cruckton Hall School

(Founded 1981)

Cruckton Hall, Cruckton, Shrewsbury, Shropshire SY5 8PR
Tel: 0743 860206 Fax: 0743 860206

Head: Mr I.D. Barrett, CertEd, Dip Special Ed
Age range: 8-16. Boarders from 8
No. of pupils enrolled as at 1.1.92: 40
Fees per annum: Boarding £25,200

Type: Emotionally and behaviourally disturbed (EBD)

Religious denomination: Inter denominational

Member of: AWMNMISS

Curriculum: With an overall ratio of nearly one to one we can give the boys their most important need - individual time. The generous staffing ratio is used to enable each boy's problems to be identified and individual programmes incorporated within the wide curriculum that is provided. We enable the boys to experience success, self esteem, and a sense of achievement, whether that means acquiring the basic everyday skills required for survival in society, or a series of good external examination results.

Participation within the community is fostered, and the boys are not encouraged to feel special or unusual. We have links with local schools, the College of Further Education, Army Cadets, Youth Clubs, Work Experience, Community Service, the local Careers Office and a multitude of various sporting bodies.

Entry requirements: Placement Officers or other Authority representatives are invited to contact the School and visit prior to an application for placement being made. Joint interviews for pupil, parent and school will be offered where vacancies exist.

Examinations offered: English, Maths, Science (common core), Design & Realisation (Wood), Home Economics, Motor Vehicle studies, Computer studies, History, Geography, Art & Craft.

Academic and leisure facilities: Classrooms and specialist rooms, Sports Hall, playing fields and woods.

Cruckton Hall is a residential school for boys experiencing emotional and behavioural difficulties, and provides a full educational programme within a structured, caring community. The School is fully registered and recognised by the Department of Education and Science, and enjoys a national reputation for success.

Farney Close School

(Founded 1946)

**Bolney Court, Bolney,
West Sussex RH17 5RD
Tel: 0444 881 811 Fax: 0444 881 957**

Head: Rod Thompson, BEd(Hons)
(Member of NAHT, AWMC, NCB)
Age range: 8-17
No. of pupils enrolled as at 1.1.92:
50 Boys 25 Girls
Fees per annum: Boarding: c. £22,290
52 week: +£9212

Type: Group 2(s) Mixed Residential EBD

Curriculum: We offer a curriculum which complies with the requirements of the National Curriculum, setting the structure and flexibility which allows for growth and development of the individual pupil. Our social and residential practice aims at securing a safe, but stimulating environment. We cater for children for whom mainstream schooling has been an unhappy experience. We encourage children to develop at their right pace and do not attempt to force our pupils into stero-typed moulds. We respect their individuality and build on positive attributes, no matter how tenuous they may seem.

Entry requirements: Our pupils are statemented under the 1981 Ed Act. Usually our referrals are made via Local Education Authorities. We always try to meet new candidates on their 'home turf' before they visit the school.

Examinations offered: A range of GCSE examinations with AEB Basic skills, and City & Guilds Foundation Courses covering a wide area, for less academic pupils. We also offer a variety of work experience and community service placements.

Academic and leisure facilities: Educational and social care arrangements are carried out in age-appropriate styles and settings. Our classroom facilities accommodate a full range of academic subjects. We have a magnificent modern sports hall. We are located on a 37 acre estate with woods, parkland and a lake. We encourage pupils to take part in community based activities such as Scouts, Guides, Cadets, athletics and football.

We offer a range of support services to children with the aim of creating a therapeutic milieu, and are able to offer 52 week care to suitable clients.

PROSPECTUSES
MINI-PROSPECTUSES
NEWSLETTERS
EXHIBITION MATERIALS
MARKETING
VIDEO FILMS
SCHOOL MAGAZINES
SCHOOL YEAR BOOKS

John Catt Educational Limited

Great Glemham
Saxmundham
Suffolk IP17 2DH

Tel. 0728 78 666
Fax 0728 78 415

JOHN CATT EDUCATIONAL LIMITED

Greystone House School

(Founded 1974)

*Priestclose Lane, Great Strickland,
Penrith, Cumbria CA10 3DJ
Tel: 0931 2300*

Head:Mr Brian M.J. McCarthy, BEd,
Diploma in the Education of Children with Special Needs.
(Recently was Headteacher of an LEA maintained Special School which gained national recognition through the coveted Schools Curriculum Award 1990. A testimonial is available to parents)
Age range: 11-16. Boarders from 11
No. of pupils enrolled as at 1.1.92: 14; Junior: 6 Boys; Senior: 8 Boys
Fees per annum: LEA Funded - £19,900

Type: Independent Boarding School for Boys with emotional/behavioural difficulties (Secondary disabilities may include: asthma, eczema, continence problems, obesity, mild anorexia, petit mal epilepsy, communication difficulties)

Religious denomination: None. A broadly Christian ethos prevails

Curriculum: National Curriculum offered for pupils in Y7 to Y11 inclusive. The School is taking part in national pilot of assessment arrangements for Mathematics and Science at the end of key stage three. Remedial programmes available for pupils with gaps in learning, using direct instructional techniques. Vocational programmes offered including work experience placements. Comprehensive outdoor education programme including swimming, canoeing, sailing, fell walking, caving, rock climbing and camping. Strong links with local community well established including links with local schools. This enables boys to join local groups, *eg* the Penrith Chess Club, and the Penrith Swimming Club. Records of achievement and personal action plans give pupils opportunities to gain success in academic, social, aesthetic and physical spheres.

The School is very small and is therefore able to offer a unique family ethos in which the boys enjoy closer relationships with a small number of staff. Insecurity is quickly replaced by a feeling of well-being and self-confidence. Psychiatric oversight is available and a variety of therapies are used.

Entry requirements: Pupils will be offered places subject to a referral by the LEA. All pupils are the subjects of statements of special educational need. A privately funded placement may be available. All pupils and parents are invited for interview before a decision is made.

Examinations offered: Associated Examining Board basic tests. GCSE. There is an impressive track record of examination success. Pupils also gain awards through sporting bodies and Duke of Edinburgh Award Scheme.

Academic and leisure facilities: Three

classrooms (two in a converted barn on the main school site, and one comprising a 17th century village schoolroom in Little Strickland), a workshop and two acres of outdoor play facilities. The School also uses the local sports hall at Shap twice a week and the swimming baths at Penrith. The School has its own minibus which broadens the scope of leisure opportunities. A variety of in-house resources are available to facilitate individual choice of activity including bicycles, skateboards, footballs, cricket equipment, snooker, computers, television and video player/recorder, electronic keyboards.

The School is located in spectacular countryside. The Head and his wife, Brian and Ann McCarthy, are the primary carers.

Don't forget to make use of the Reader Enquiry Service cards at the back of the Guide if you want more information about the Schools or Colleges listed.

Authoritative articles covering many important aspects of Special Learning Needs appear at the start of the Guide. Parents are urged to read them.

We specialise in consultancy, design, production and publication of:

- ☑ **Prospectuses**
- ☑ **Mini-prospectuses**
- ☑ **Newsletters**
- ☑ **Exhibition Materials**
- ☑ **Marketing**
- ☑ **Video Films**
- ☑ **School Magazines**
- ☑ **School Year Books**

Our experience and quality of craftsmanship enable us to give a service which we believe is unequalled by any other organisation at a highly competitive price.

For more details please telephone or write to:

John Catt Educational Limited
Great Glemham,
Saxmundham,
Suffolk IP17 2DH
Tel: 0728 78 666   Fax: 0728 78 415

High Close School

(Founded)

*Wiltshire Road,
Wokingham,
Berkshire RG11 1TT
Tel: 0734 785767
Fax: 0734 894220*

Principal: Mr A. Paterson, DPE, DRemEd
(Member of Assoc. of Workers with Malad. Children,
Nat. Assoc. for Remedial Ed.)
Age range: 9-16. Boarders from 9
No. of pupils enrolled as at 1.1.92: 52
Junior: 3 Boys; Senior: 38 Boys, 11 Girls
Fees per annum: Day: £13,480
Boarding: £26,961

Type: Emotionally and Behaviourally disturbed children

Religious denomination: None

Member of: AWMC, NARE

Curriculum: The curriculum encompasses all the core subjects of the National Curriculum. Individual education programmes are compiled for every child and emphasis is placed on meeting the child's own needs, whether they be at remedial or examination level. The importance of consistency across campus is stressed and residential social workers assist in school and help young people with homework in the evenings.

Entry requirements: High Close caters for boys and girls who have had unhappy educational experiences and have emotional and behavioural difficulties. Our only entry requirement is that they should wish to attend High Close and that we have preferably two years to work with a child.

Examinations offered: High Close offers exam courses in English, Arithmetic, Child Care, Art & Craft and Home Economics. We are also actively involved in the Berkshire Youth Award Scheme which has been specifically designed for young people with special needs.

We have a well developed work experience programme.

Academic and leisure facilities: We have a large campus which has five houses which cater for ten young people and five RSWs staff each of these cottages. There are spacious grounds with a tennis court and soccer pitch. The School is also very close to the centre of Wokingham and near to Reading and Bracknell. The School building is a modern purpose-built building with adequate space for classes of eight or less and is well equipped with sports equipment, computers and modern classroom furniture. We also have a well maintained, attractive and well used library. Our teaching staff comprises of a Head of Education, 11 teachers and five Teacher's Aides.

Religious activities: High Close has a mixed client group with both sexes and young people from different cultural backgrounds.

We openly acknowledge all our young people's backgrounds and have worked hard to establish an appropriate ethos on campus that enables us to become more racially and culturally aware. This stance is shown in our staff group which reflects our client group.

As part of the Barnardo's organisation, we have a well developed and highly trained staff group committed to providing high quality care and education. We have working policies on open access, child protection, care and control and are following closely the requirements of the Children Act 1989.

All our young people have six-monthly reviews and we have a well organised leave programme that enables most young people to be taken home every second weekend.

To assist this, our RSW staff and Field Social Work staff work closely with parents.

High Close is served by both a Consultant Educational Psychologist and a Psychiatrist and has the full resources of the Barnardo's organisation behind it.

The Marchant-Holliday School

North Cheriton,
Nr Templecombe,
Somerset BA8 0AH
Tel: 0963 33234

Head: Mr J.M. Robertson, BEd, DipEd
Age range: 6-13. Boarders from 6
No. of pupils enrolled as at 1.1.92: 37
Fees per annum: £17,200

Type: Charity Independent Residential for Boys with emotional and behavioural difficulties. DES Approved.

Religious denomination: Non-denominational

Curriculum: The National Curriculum. Children are taught by experienced teachers in class groups of no more than eight. A broad curriculum is provided with emphasis on foundation subjects and meeting individual needs. Facilities and resources are of the highest standard and children are encouraged to fulfil their potential for social and academic growth. Sufficient progress is often made to facilitate reintegration into mainstream schooling. There are excellent sporting and recreational facilities and a wide range of out of school activities are offered. The School provides high quality care and a warm and homely atmosphere. The matron is a qualified nurse.

Entry requirements: By interview at School.

Muntham House School

(Founded 1953)

*Barns Green,
Horsham,
West Sussex RH13 7NJ
Tel: 0403 730302 Fax: 0403 730501*

Head: Mr A.G. Train, MEd, BA, CertEd
Age range: 8-19. Boarders from 8
No. of pupils enrolled as at 1.1.92: 38
Junior: 13; Senior: 21; Sixth Form: 4
Fees per annum: Boarding £16,695
Sixth Form Boarding: £21,930

Type: Residential non-maintained Special School for Boys with emotional/behavioural problems

Religious denomination: Non-denominational

Curriculum: Broad curriculum. Small classes. Facility to progress to external examinations. One-to-one provision available for counselling/therapy; structured approach in Main School. Three age groupings: Primary, Secondary and F.E. Highly Specialised, with appropriate staffing and facilities.

Entry requirements: Usually through Statementing Procedure; but by direct approach to Headmaster. Central aetiology: emotional problems and associated behavioural and learning difficulties.

PROSPECTUSES
MINI-PROSPECTUSES
NEWSLETTERS
EXHIBITION MATERIALS
MARKETING
VIDEO FILMS
SCHOOL MAGAZINES
SCHOOL YEAR BOOKS

John Catt Educational Limited

Great Glemham
Saxmundham
Suffolk IP17 2DH

Tel: 0728 78 666
Fax: 0728 78 415

JOHN CATT EDUCATIONAL LIMITED

Nugent House School

(Founded 1983)

*Carr Mill Road,
Billinge, Nr Wigan,
Lancashire WN5 7TT
Tel: 0744 892551
Fax: 0744 895697*

Head: Mr C.G. Mills, MA, DipEd, CertEd
Age range: 8-17. Boarders from 8
No. of pupils enrolled as at 1.1.92:
Junior: 15; Senior: 60; Sixth Form: 3
Fees per annum: Day: £11,930.04
Boarding: £17,895.00

Type: Special Needs Associated with Emotional and Behavioural Problems. Also a small unit catering for children with a history of psychiatric disorders.

Religious denomination: Roman Catholic Foundation with Interdenominational Intake

Member of: Liverpool Catholic Social Services

Curriculum: A full range of educational abilities exists within the School population and therefore whilst remedial help is available for those with specific learning difficulties, a full public examination programme is also offered. The School meets the National Curriculum requirements of the Education Reform Act 1988 and curriculum development continues as the requirement of the legislation come into force. All fifth year boys undertake a Leavers Programme consisting of Careers Education, Work Experience and Life and Social Skills Training.

Entry requirements: Normally by virtue of a Statement of Special Educational Needs. However, some children are accepted whilst in the process of assessment.

St Edward's School

(Founded 1963)

*Melchet Court, Sherfield English,
Romsey,
Hampshire SO51 6ZR
Tel: 0794 884271*

Head: Mr D.J. Doyle, BEd (Member of AIRSS)
Age range: 10-16+. Boarders from 10
No. of pupils enrolled as at 1.9.91: 90
Lower: 30 Boys; Middle: 30 Boys; Senior: 30 Boys
Fees per annum: Boarding: £22,140

Type: Special Residential for emotionally and behaviourally disturbed, and Specific Learning Difficulties

Religious denomination: Catering for all denominations

Member of: AIRSS, NABC, HABC

Curriculum: The School follows the National Curriculum, and its organization for Education corresponds to that for Care by having three year groups.

Lower School (ages 10-14) *ie* Year 6-9, have a very wide variety of learning experiences covering 19 subjects, emphasis being placed on core subjects with specialist assistance for boys with learning difficulties.

Middle School (ages 14-15) Year 10, have three double periods of Mathematics and English every week, and also Science, Information Technology, Physical Education, Personal and Social Education, Design Technology, Games, Drama and Integrated Humanities.

Senior School (ages 15-16) Year 11, follow GCSE courses in many of the above subjects to all GCSE levels, and select one of the vocational courses in Carpentry & Joinery, Painting & Decorating, Brickwork or Horticulture, taken to City & Guilds level. From September 1992 pupils will follow pre-16 NVQ courses.

Entry requirements: Applications for places to The Headmaster.

Examinations offered: GCSE courses of four examining boards and City & Guilds Skills Tests in a vocational subject. Certificate of the Construction Industry Training Board.

Academic and leisure facilities: In addition to the very broad curriculum, a comprehensive educational and personality assessment by our Consultant Child & Educational Psychologist, Dr R.M. Griffiths (ex HMI Special Needs Inspector) is offered free to authorities wishing to avail themselves of the service. The school is renowned for its wide range of sporting and social activities which take place at weekends and evenings throughout the year. The activities are too numerous to list in full, but they include: Motor-cycling, Quad Bikes, Motor Mechanics, Sub-Aqua Club, Horse-riding, Canoeing, Home Economics, Model-making, Weight-training, Computers, Swimming, Roller Hockey, Gymnastics, Football, Badminton, Basketball, Art and Drama.

An extensive Summer Camp programme complements the leisure activities. The week long camps include Outward-Bound activities in Devon; Cycling, Canoeing and Hiking on the Isle of Wight; walking in the Yorkshire Dales; Pony-riding in the New Forest, and Fishing on the River Nene, Peterborough.

Don't forget to make use of the Reader Enquiry Service cards at the back of the Guide if you want more information about the Schools or Colleges listed.

South Lodge School

(Founded 1978)

*High Street,
Baldock,
Hertfordshire SG7 6BX
Tel: 0462 892715*

Head: Mrs Rita Kirkwood, BSc, MSc, DipSpEd
Age range: 12-18. Boarders from 12
No. of pupils enrolled as at 1.1.92: 26
Fees per week: Boarding £799

Type: Residential special School EBD. Special Educational Needs.

Member of: Social Care Association

Curriculum: The School follows the National Curriculum. AEB Basic exams or GCSEs are taken as appropriate. BTec Foundation, College, YT, Work experience and a 16+ unit all contribute towards independent living. Holidays, outward bound, sailing, abseiling, swimming, riding, skating, reflexology, jewellery making, gardening, drama, theatre visits etc. 52 or 42 week placements. Structured care programme.

Entry requirements: Referrals from Social Service Depts or Education Authorities.

Spinney School

(Founded 1959)

*Little London,
Heathfield,
East Sussex TN21 0NU
Tel: 0435 866304*

Principal: T.P. O'Hare
Head Teacher: Mrs I. Woodward
Age range: 10-17. Boarders from 10-17
No. of pupils enrolled as at 1.1.92:
Junior: 5; Senior: 14;
Sixth Form: 3
Fees per annum:
Day: £7950; Boarding: £19,395
Sixth Form: Day £8988, Boarding: £21,930
Present fee increase for January not finalised.

Type: Residential School for Boys with emotional and behavioural difficulties

Religious denomination: None

Member of: AWMC, SCA

Curriculum: The School's objective is to produce the best scheme of work to meet a boy's individual needs, to build confidence and self-esteem so that he makes progress and to encourage those who have had little success in earlier schools. A full curriculum is offered, with reference to the National Curriculum, but also being aware of possible individual limitations. External Exams: City & Guilds, BTec and AEB, and the school is a registered GCSE centre. Sixth Form: an extra year allowing an extension of studies, day release CPVE course at a local college, and development of social and independent living skills.

PROSPECTUSES
MINI-PROSPECTUSES
NEWSLETTERS
EXHIBITION MATERIALS
MARKETING
VIDEO FILMS
SCHOOL MAGAZINES
SCHOOL YEAR BOOKS

John Catt Educational Limited

Great Glemham
Saxmundham
Suffolk IP17 2DH

Tel: 0728 78 666
Fax: 0728 78 415

JOHN CATT EDUCATIONAL LIMITED

Sydney House Communities

(Founded 1979)

14 Domneva Road,
Westgate-on-Sea,
Kent CT8 8PE
Tel: 0843 31346 Fax: 0843 823386

Heads: Paul Spens and Lianne Gentle
Age range: 12-16. Boarders from 12
No. of pupils enrolled as at 1.1.92: 11 maximum
6 Boys 5 Girls
Fees per week: Boarding: £1062

Type: Co-educational Psychotherapeutic Community for severely emotionally disturbed adolescents

Religious denomination: None

Member of: National Association of Therapeutic Communities

Curriculum: Mainstream/core curriculum, modified, ranging from remedial/compensatory to GCSE. 50% 1:1 tuition. Multi disciplinary team teaching, sympathetic to and supportive of psycho-therapy, work experience/life skills emphasised and strong links with further educational resources.

Normal curriculum schools with facilities to help pupils with Dyslexia or Special Learning Needs appear in Section Four.

Authoritative articles covering many important aspects of Special Learning Needs appear at the start of the Guide. Parents are urged to read them.

Tregynon Hall

(Founded January 1988)

*Tregynon,
Newtown,
Powys SY16 3PG
Tel: 0686 87 330*

Head: Mrs M.E. Holmes, BA(Hons), ATC/AT
Age range: 9-18. Boarders from all ages
No. of pupils enrolled as at 1.1.92: 23
Junior: 9 Boys; Senior: 10 Boys 4 Girls
Fees: £55 per day Education
£57.50 per day care

Type: Emotional & Behavioural Difficulties

Curriculum: Full age appropriate curriculum based upon National Curriculum recommendations.

We specialise in consultancy, design, production and publication of:

- ☑ **Prospectuses**
- ☑ **Mini-prospectuses**
- ☑ **Newsletters**
- ☑ **Exhibition Materials**
- ☑ **Marketing**
- ☑ **Video Films**
- ☑ **School Magazines**
- ☑ **School Year Books**

Our experience and quality of craftsmanship enable us to give a service which we believe is unequalled by any other organisation at a highly competitive price.

John Catt Educational Limited
Great Glemham,
Saxmundham,
Suffolk IP17 2DH
Tel: 0728 78 666 Fax: 0728 78 415

West Kirby Residential School

(Founded 1890)

*Meols Drive,
West Kirby, Wirral,
Merseyside L48 5DH
Tel: 051 632 3201*

Head: Mr T.I.F. Price, BEd(Hons), DipSpecEd, CertEd
Age range: 8-16+. Boarders from 8
No. of pupils enrolled as at 1.1.92: 70
Junior: 19 Boys 11 Girls; Senior: 25 Boys 15 Girls
Fees per annum: On application

Type: Non-Maintained Special School - Residential and Day.

Religious denomination: Non denominational

Member of: NAIMS, NCSE

Curriculum: Full access to National Curriculum. Junior and Senior Departments. Individual programmes for the less able (Class sizes 6/10 pupils). GCSE English, English Literature, Maths, Science, History, Geography, Art and Craft, Home Economics. Leavers' Programmes, Link Courses, IT facility, wide selection of out of school activities. Small living groups. Full nursing care if required.

Entry requirements: Applications via LEA. Children with Special Educational Needs - PH, Diabetic, Epileptic etc, EBD and MLD.

Display Listings of normal curriculum
Schools and Colleges offering
Learning Support

Bethany School

(Founded 1866)

*Curtisden Green,
Goudhurst, Cranbrook,
Kent TN17 1LB
Tel: 0580 211273 Fax: 0580 211151*

Headmaster: Mr W.M. Harvey, MA
Age range: 11-18. Boarders from 11
No. of pupils enrolled as at 1.9.91: 270
Senior: 276 Boys 3 Girls; Sixth Form: 60 Boys
Fees per annum: Day: £1636-£1720
Boarding: £2556-£2640

Type: Co-educational Senior Independent Day and Boarding School. Dyslexia and Learning Support Department.

Religious denomination: Church of England

Member of: SHMIS, BSA, GBA, Bursars Association

Curriculum: A broad curriculum is followed leading to GCSE and GCE A level. Most pupils remain for the strong Sixth Form, where there are opportunities to follow examination courses in Business Studies, Sports Studies and Photography as well as 14 other A level subjects.

Entry requirements: The School has its own termly Entry Test (Mathematics, English and IQ tests). Sixth Form entry - by interview and GCSE results.

PROSPECTUSES
MINI-PROSPECTUSES
NEWSLETTERS
EXHIBITION MATERIALS
MARKETING
VIDEO FILMS
SCHOOL MAGAZINES
SCHOOL YEAR BOOKS

John Catt Educational Limited
Great Glemham
Saxmundham
Suffolk IP17 2DH

Tel 0728 78 666
Fax 0728 78 415

JOHN CATT EDUCATIONAL LIMITED

Bryn Alyn Community

(Founded 1968)

*Head Office,
Llay Road, Old Rhosrobin,
Wrexham,
Clwyd LL11 4RL
Tel: 0978 355757 Fax: 0978 264720*

Principals:
North Wales: Glyn Condliffe, BA, CertEd, ACP (Sp Nds);
Shropshire: Mike Melaniphy, BEd (8.13) Ord, BEd (Hons) Sp Ed Needs
Age range: 11-16. Boarders from 11-16
No. of pupils enrolled as at 1.1.92:
North Wales: 65 Shropshire: 30
Fees per week: Boarding: £750

Type: Two Residential Special Schools (Education Act 1981, Sections 11(3)(a) and 13(2)): One School in North Wales and one in Shropshire.

Religious denomination: None

Member of: AWMC, SCA, NCB

Curriculum: A wide and flexible curriculum is offered in attempt to meet a wide range of need. The National Curriculum is offered in English, Mathematics and Science.

Entry requirements: All children and young people referred to the Community are considered according to their individual need.

Examinations offered: AEB Skills Tests; GCSE; RSA; City and Guilds.

Academic and leisure facilities: Academic facilities include the use of computers. The

Schools offer the opportunity to either pursue an academic programme or a more practical-based programme. An extensive range of leisure time facilities from dry slope skiing to football and other outdoor pursuits to Drama.

Chelmsford Hall

(Founded 1920)

71 Carlisle Road, Eastbourne,
East Sussex BN20 7EL
Tel: 0323 34261

Head: David G. Stevens, MA
Age range: 6½ - 14. Boarders from 6½
No of pupils enrolled as at 1.1.92: 90
Range of fees per annum (incl VAT) as at 1.1.92:
Day: £2700-£3750; Boarding: £6375
Specialist Tuition: £1950-£4050

Type: Preparatory School

Religious affiliation: Inter-denominational but all faiths welcome

Member of: IAPS

Curriculum: The School provides a broad curriculum for the individual in preparation for entry to the next school, and for adult life.

Entry requirements: Entry is by interview, plus an Educational Psychologist's assessment if available.

Academic and leisure facilities: The caring family atmosphere together with small classes and specialist tuition enable children to enjoy school and gain confidence through achievement. The School has designed a language development programme which is suitable for specific learning difficulties, also known as dyslexia, mild dyspraxics, mild dysphasics and late starters. There is a large qualified staff to cater for the educational and pastoral needs of these children both in and out of the classroom.

The School provides for day, weekly and full boarding placements, and parental access is encouraged. There is an escorted train or coach service between Eastbourne and London Victoria at long weekend and half-term visits home. The School is situated in a premier seaside resort with easy access to the countryside.

COUNSELLING

For professional guidance on educational matters, we should be glad to arrange an appointment with a consultant for a nominal fee.

For further details, please contact Richard Leathes, our senior consultant.

★ School, College, Sixth Form
★ Choice of GCSE/A Level Subjects
★ Degree course applications
★ Career options

GABBITAS TRUMAN & THRING

6, 7 & 8 Sackville Street, Piccadilly,
London W1X 2BR

Telephone: 071-734 0161 Telex: 28707
Fax: 071-437 1764

Consultants on Independent Education since 1873

Edgarley Hall
(Millfield Junior School)

(Founded 1946)

*Glastonbury,
Somerset BA6 8LD
Tel: 0458 32446 Fax: 0458 33679*

Headmaster: Richard J Smyth, MA, CertEd
Age range: 8-13. Boarders from 8
No. of pupils enrolled as at 1.1.92: 484
248 Boys 236 Girls
Fees per annum:
Day: £1610; Boarding: £2585

Type: Preparatory, Co-educational, Boarding and Day School. All Specific Learning Difficulties catered for.

Religious denomination: Interdenominational - Christian

Member of: IAPS, ISIS. The Bath Assoc. for the Study of Dyslexia. Somerset Dyslexia Assoc.

Curriculum: Pupils are taught mainly by their class teacher until the age of 10. The curriculum remains broad with all pupils studying art, craft, technology and music throughout the School. Specialist staff and small teaching groups ensure that pupils learn at a pace that suits individual needs. Specialist help is provided by our Language Development Centre for pupils with Specific Learning Difficulties.

Entry requirements: Entry is by interview and a report from the present school, or by the Bursary Examination set in November.

Authoritative articles covering many important aspects of Special Learning Needs appear at the start of the Guide. Parents are urged to read them.

Ellough School

*The Grange,
Church Road,
Ellough, Beccles,
Suffolk NR34 7TR
Tel: 0502 711739*

Head: C G Stewart, BSc
Age range: 7-13. Boarders from 7-13
No. of pupils enrolled as at 1.1.92: 18
Boys 15 Girls 3
Range of fees per annum (incl VAT) as at 1.1.92:
Day: £6375 Boarding: £8325

Type: Learning Difficulties / Dyslexia

Religious affiliation: Interdenominational

Ellough School offers a full curriculum with all lessons taught in such a way as to make them accessible to dyslexic children. Individual lessons in addition to the normal timetable address the needs of each child. There is a programme of afternoon activities and there is a physical games session each day. There are no compulsory extras.

A full range of guides to UK Schools is also published by John Catt Educational.

Edington School

(Founded 1974)

*Mark Road,
Burtle, Bridgwater,
Somerset TA7 8NJ
Tel: 0278 722 012*

Headmaster: G Nickerson, CertEd
Age range: 8-13. Boarders from 8
No. of pupils enrolled as at 1.1.92:
104 Boys   6 Girls
Fees per annum: Day: £4761
Boarding: £7847

Type: Preparatory School

Religious denomination: Non denominational

Member of: IAPS

Curriculum: Edington is for children with specific learning difficulties (dyslexia). A pupil will follow a programme specifically designed to meet and overcome his/her language or numeracy difficulties.

The skills required are taught by trained and sympathetic staff and it is hoped with their help the child will develop the all important self confidence, self respect, self discipline and individuality which he/she earnestly seeks.

To supplement these important skills the School follows a traditional prep school programme, incorporating the relevant areas of the National Curriculum geared to the pupils language numeracy level and ability. The syllabus includes the following ability subjects: English, handwriting, keyboard skills, library work, maths, science, humanities, art, woodwork, music, divinity, computer studies, physical education and games.

Teaching groups vary from 5 - 12 in number and there are the all important individual lessons in English and Maths for pupils who need extra help. A speech and language therapist is available for children who require therapy.

The entry requirements are an Educational Psychologist's report, an interview with the Headmaster and at least an average IQ.

The principal games are cricket, rugby, soccer, athletics and swimming. The school also offers an extremely wide range of extra curricular activities including a thriving Brass Band.

Edington pupils attend church every Sunday.

Shapwick School

(Founded 1981)

*Shapwick Manor,
Shapwick, Nr Bridgwater,
Somerset TA7 9NJ
Tel: 0458 210384*

Joint Headmasters: D.C. Walker, BA (Hons), CertEd
J.P. Whittock, CertEd
Age range: 13-17
No. of pupils enrolled as at 1.9.91:
96 Boys   3 Girls
Fees per annum:
Day: £4998; Boarding: £8433

Type: Senior School

Religious denomination: Non denominational

Member of: ISAI

Curriculum: Shapwick, Edington's sister school, shares the same aims as Edington and continues the education of its pupils to GCSE. The curriculum is designed to offer a wide range of subjects that can make maximum demands on the students' strengths whilst the teaching supports students' learning difficulties in every lesson.

All students follow a common curriculum in the 3rd Year, and very importantly as well as offering a broad spread of curricular areas, study skills and keyboard skills are incorporated.

As well as having specialist staff to assist students with their literacy and numeracy difficulties, all staff are experienced and trained in the techniques necessary to help dyslexics achieve. Most students take six or seven subjects including English Language and Mathematics. Choices are made from Biology, Chemistry, Physics, Computer studies, Geography, History, Design, Technology, Art, Literature and French.

A wide variety of team and individual games is available, both to increase skills and for recreation. There is a wide range of clubs and activities available after school. There are several trips arranged in this country and overseas each year. The School offers careers advice and work experience. All pupils are encouraged to take part in the Duke of Edinburgh Award Scheme.

Entry requirements are an Educational Psychologist's Report diagnosing specific learning difficulties and at least average potential, a current Headmaster's Report, and an interview.

Grenville College

(Founded 1954)

Belvoir Road, Bideford, Devon EX39 3JR
Tel: 0237 472212

Head: Dr M.C.V. Cane, BSc, PhD, MRSC
Age range: 10-18
No. of pupils enrolled as at 1.1.92: 330
(Sixth Form: 68)
Fees per term: Day: £1302
Junior Boarders (under 13): £2618;
Senior Boarders (13+): £2655

Type: Independent Boys Secondary Boarding & Day, with a Unit catering for Specific Learning Difficulties/Dyslexia

Religious denomination: Church of England

Member of: SHMIS, GBA, Western Division Woodard Schools

Curriculum: With 43 teachers of academic subjects in a school of 330 pupils our classes are small. 24 GCSE courses are available and 18 A level courses. All the musical instruments are taught, and a good number of boys take the instrumental music grade examinations with success.

Entry requirements: An up-to-date Educational Psychologist's report to be sent to the School prior to a boy's interview and testing at Grenville. All entrants are expected to be of at least average intelligence and capable of following academic courses to GCSE level.

Subject specialities and academic track record: Science subjects, electronics, computer studies, craft-design. Oxbridge entry achievable. A famous and a fully integrated dyslexia unit for English skills for boys with genuine academic potential. The Unit has a Director and five full-time and three part-time staff.

Examinations offered: GCSE and A levels,

John Catt Educational Limited

We specialise in consultancy, design, production and publication of:

- ☑ Prospectuses
- ☑ Mini-prospectuses
- ☑ Newsletters
- ☑ Exhibition Materials
- ☑ Marketing
- ☑ Video Films
- ☑ School Magazines
- ☑ School Year Books

Our experience and quality of craftsmanship enable us to give a service which we believe is unequalled by any other organisation at a highly competitive price.

John Catt Educational Limited
Great Glemham,
Saxmundham,
Suffolk IP17 2DH
Tel: 0728 78 666 Fax: 0728 78 415

Midland, Southern, Northern GCSEs. Oxford, AEB, JMB A levels.

Boys go on to universities, medical schools, polytechnics; to Sandhurst and Dartmouth, to agricultural colleges, to vocational courses in commercial art, catering and hotel management.

Academic and leisure facilities include: Well-equipped Science laboratories, a language laboratory, excellent Craft/Design and Art facilities. Computer and electronics departments, extensive playing fields, swimming pool and gymnasium. Miniature rifle range and 100 metre open range, 10 tennis courts, all-weather hockey pitch. 14 school sports and 29 clubs. Dinghies, canoes, and wind-surfing.

Curriculum: Everybody follows a core to ensure cultural continuity, but modifications are devised to cater for specific needs. For example, extra English can be substituted for French and Latin. The basic importance of ENGLISH and MATHS are always at the front of the minds of all the staff, and half the time in school is spent on these. Individuals and groups come out of class to specialist tutors who work closely with the Dyslexia Association. We value the individual effort of the pupil and do not set one up against the other.

Entry requirements: Assessment and reports.

Hillcroft Preparatory School

(Founded 1911)

*Walnutree Manor,
Haughley Green, Stowmarket,
Suffolk IP14 3RQ
Tel: 0449 673003*

Head: Mr F.R.G.J. Rapsey, BEd (Hons), ACP, FRSA, FSA (Scot), FCollP
Mrs G.O. Rapsey, CertEd
Age range: 2½-13. Boarders from 8 (exceptionally 7)
No. of pupils enrolled as at 1.1.92: 140
70 Boys 70 Girls
Fees per annum: Day: £960 (babes) - £3300
Boarding: £1800

Type: Co-educational Preparatory School (Dyslexia, remedial, emotional problems, psychological problems particularly cared for). Emotional/behavioural difficulties.

Religious denomination: Church of England, but all sincere beliefs welcomed

Member of: ISAI, BSA, NAHT, AHIS, ISIS

We specialise in consultancy, design, production and publication of:

- ☑ **Prospectuses**
- ☑ **Mini-prospectuses**
- ☑ **Newsletters**
- ☑ **Exhibition Materials**
- ☑ **Marketing**
- ☑ **Video Films**
- ☑ **School Magazines**
- ☑ **School Year Books**

Our experience and quality of craftsmanship enable us to give a service which we believe is unequalled by any other organisation at a highly competitive price.

John Catt Educational Limited
Great Glemham,
Saxmundham,
Suffolk IP17 2DH
Tel: 0728 78 666   Fax: 0728 78 415

A full range of guides to UK Schools is also published by John Catt Educational.

Moon Hall School

(Founded 1985)

*Belmont School,
Feldemore,
Holmbury St Mary,
Dorking, Surrey RH5 6LQ
Tel: 0306 731464*

Head: Mrs B.E. Baker, BA, PGCE
(Member of AMBDA)
Age range: 7-13.
Boarders from 7-13 (Weekly Mon-Fri only)
No. of pupils enrolled as at 1.1.92: 61
52 Boys 9 Girls
Fees per annum: Day: £1505-£2395
Boarding: £2240-£3130

Type: A Co-educational School for intelligent dyslexic children in the grounds of Belmont Prep School.

Religious denomination: Christian - all denominations

Member of: ISIS, Corporate Member of British Dyslexia Association

Curriculum: The usual subjects are taught plus CDT, Music, Art, IT and Drama. Each child is treated as an individual. There is specialist English and Maths teaching and classes where the curriculum is adapted for dyslexic children. Flexible integration with Belmont School allows older children to do a full CE course if appropriate with support in English and Maths. A PE and sports programme is provided together with clubs and activities. We aim to give children the advantages of a mainstream prep school plus specialist expertise.

Entry requirements: Report from educational psychologist, interview and school assessment.

GABBITAS TRUMAN AND THRING

GUARDIANSHIP

We offer a comprehensive guardianship service to overseas parents whose children are at boarding school in the UK. We find a suitable guardian family to look after your child during half-terms, exeat weekends and holidays. The guardian families keep in close contact with our department and their commitment is to the welfare of your child.

For details contact Sarah Studdert-Kennedy of the Guardianship Department

**The Gabbitas, Truman & Thring
Educational Trust,
6 – 8 Sackville Street, Piccadilly,
London W1X 2BR**

**Telephone: 071-734 0161
or 071-439 2071**

**Fax: 071-437 1764
Telex: 28707 GABTAS G**

Authoritative articles covering many important aspects of Special Learning Needs appear at the start of the Guide. Parents are urged to read them.

Queen Ethelburga's College

(Founded 1912)

*Thorpe Underwood Hall,
Ouseburn, York YO5 9SZ
Tel: 0423 330711 Fax: 0423 331007*

Head: Mrs J.M. Town, BA (Oxon)
(Member of JMB, GSA)
Age range: Girls & Boys 2½-11, Girls only 11-18
No. of pupils enrolled as at 1.1.92: 300
Junior: 11 Boys 109 Girls; Senior: 180
Fees per annum:
Junior: Day £685- £995, Boarding £2275
Senior: Day £1595, Boarding £2475

Type: Day, Weekly or Full Boarding - Girls & Boys 2½ -11, Girls only 11-18

Religious denomination: Church of England, but all denominations accepted.

Member of: GSA, HMC, GBSA

Curriculum: Pupils with specific learning difficulties study the National Curriculum with the other pupils, but receive support in subjects where needed. Problems are assessed and pupils are given help individually and in small groups to help them manage their problems. Qualified and experienced special needs staff provide multi-sensory tuition and liaise with the subject staff to help these pupils achieve their maximum potential success and happiness. Fully qualified Dyslexic Institute staff.

Entry requirements: Assessment taken on a day spent in school plus an interview. Sight of Educational Psychologists report preferable.

Examinations offered: Common Entrance at 11+, 12+, 13+, GCSE AS, and A level courses. Business/Office Information Course, Typing, City and Guilds Information Technology Diploma.

Academic and leisure facilities: Over £5,500,00 spent on new facilities which include three science laboratories, three computer rooms, Art and Design Centre, Music and Drama Centre and in 1992 an Equestrian Centre. Outdoor pursuits include Duke of Edinburgh Award Scheme, team matches in lacrosse, netball and other pursuits like canoeingm abseiling, etc.

Religious activities: Church of England pastoral care undertaken by caring qualified staff.

St David's College

(Founded 1965)

*Gloddaeth Hall,
Llandudno,
N Wales LL30 1RD
Tel: 0492 875974 Fax: 0492 870383*

Head: Mr William Seymour, MA
Age range: 11-18 . Boarders from 11-18
No. of male pupils enrolled as at 1.1.92: 210
Junior: 39 Senior: 109 Sixth Form: 62
Fees per annum: Day: £4995
Boarding: £7740

Type: Independent Mainstream Boys' School, approved by the DES for the admission of boys between the ages of 11 and 18 with moderate and specific learning difficulties (Dyslexia).

Religious denomination: Inter-denominational

Member of: SHMIS, SHA

Curriculum: St David's is a small independent mainstream school with a dyslexia unit which caters fully for its pupils by way of individual tuition on an extraction system. Specialist mainstream tuition in English is provided, and support teaching is available for other subjects. Option choices for GCSE are supervised closely and monitored throughout the courses. All classroom teachers are sympathetically aware of pupils with special needs.

Entry requirements: Entry is possible at age 11, 12 or 13, and there is a small Sixth Form entry. The procedure is an integrated process which involves an educational psychologist's assessment, a thorough interview, a report from the present Head Teacher and a loosely competitive entrance exam used mainly for placement purposes. At interview, the pupil's potential contribution to the School community in a variety of areas is an important component.

Examinations offered:
GCSE: English Language, English Literature, Mathematics, Biology, Chemistry, Physics, History, Geography, French, Spanish, Information Technology, Religious Studies, Art, CDT, Commerce, Music.
A level: English, Mathematics, Biology, Chemistry, Physics, History, Geography, French, Spanish, Business Studies, Art, History of Art, CDT.

Academic and leisure facilities: Well equipped science laboratories, computer rooms, CDT centre, art block, extensive games fields for rugby, football, hockey, cricket, tennis and athletics. Two squash courts, gymnasium, weights room, outstanding outdoor pursuits activities in Snowdonia: mountaineering, canoeing, caving, orienteering, sailing and windsurfing. Skiing trips and major expeditions abroad. A wide range of clubs and societies.

Religious activities: The Christian faith underlies the life of the school. There is an assembly each morning and a morning service on Sundays. Different age groups may attend their own Bible Study groups and boys are prepared for Confirmation each year.

PROSPECTUSES
MINI-PROSPECTUSES
NEWSLETTERS
EXHIBITION MATERIALS
MARKETING
VIDEO FILMS
SCHOOL MAGAZINES
SCHOOL YEAR BOOKS

John Catt Educational Limited
*Great Glemham
Saxmundham
Suffolk IP17 2DH*
Tel: 0728 78 666
Fax: 0728 78 415

JOHN CATT EDUCATIONAL LIMITED

GABBITAS TRUMAN AND THRING

There are a great many schools and colleges to choose from and finding the one that will be the best for your child is no easy matter. Our knowledge of the independent sector is extensive and covers all categories of schools and colleges in the UK.

For example, we can help with the choice of:

- Independent preparatory and secondary schools
- Tutorial colleges
- Domestic Science and Secretarial Colleges
- Finishing Schools in the UK and abroad
- Language courses and Schools of English

For more information on how we can help you make the right choice, telephone and ask to speak to one of our advisors, or if you prefer, write to us with as much information as possible about your child, at:

**Gabbitas, Truman & Thring Educational Trust,
6 – 8 Sackville Street, Piccadilly, London W1X 2BR**

Telephone: 071-734 0161
or 071-439 2071

Fax: 071-437 1764
Telex: 28707 GABTAS G

Sibford School

(Founded 1842)

*Sibford Ferris,
Banbury, Oxfordshire OX15 5QL
Tel: 0295 78441 Fax: 0295 788444*

Head: John Dunston, MA, AIL
Age range: 7-18. Boarders from 9
No. of pupils enrolled as at 1.1.92: 354
Junior: Boys 19 Girls 17; Senior: Boys 169 Girls 98
Sixth Form: Boys 33 Girls 18
Range of fees per term (incl VAT) as at 1.1.92:
Day: £850 - £1332 Boarding: £1950 - £2617
Sixth Form Day: £1332 Boarding: £2617

Type: Independent Boarding: full/weekly and day. Mainstream curriculum. Renowned dyslexia tuition and support for small number of pupils with other learning difficulties.

Religious affiliation:
Religious Society of Friends (Quakers)

Member of: FSJC, ISJC, BSA, GBA

Curriculum: Junior Department (age 7-10): A wide- ranging curriculum is provided to children in small groups. Literacy, numeracy, science and technology skills are emphasised alongside art, music, drama and PE. A specialist teacher helps individual children with Specific Learning Difficulties.
Main School (age 11-16): Pupils follow a full curriculum to GCSE, with an unusually broad spectrum of choices in academic, artistic and practical subjects, enabling each pupil to make the most of individual strengths. The outstanding Specific Learning Difficulties Department gives specialised daily help, and a small number of children with other learning difficulties also receive extra tuition.
Sixth Form: This offers a genuine alternative to a traditional three A level course. Students work toward the City and Guilds Diploma in Vocational Education, with the possibility of selected A level and BTEC options.

Entry requirements: Admission to the Junior Department (Orchard Close) and the Main School is by interview and internal tests, and a report from the candidate's school is required. Sixth Form places are awarded after interview and are dependent on a good report from the pupil's previous school. Dyslexic pupils require a recent Educational Psychologist's report.

Examinations offered: Main School: All pupils work towards GCSE at 16+ with a full choice of academic subjects complemented by a deliberately wide range of artistic and practical subjects in a spectrum including Art, Child Development, Drama, Food, Music, Design Communication and Realisation, Rural Studies and Textiles. Business Studies and Information Technology are important new features of the curriculum.
Sixth Form: A one or two year course. Qualifications available include the Diploma in Vocational Education, A level and BTEC First Awards.

Academic and leisure facilities:

* National known centre of excellence in Dyslexia Tuition

* Outstanding new Drama and Music facilities

* New multi-purpose Sports Centre and Squash Courts

* Well-equipped Library and three Information Technology bases

* Sibford Laptop Initiative - of particular value to special needs pupils

* Newly developed Technology Centre

* Wide range of indoor and outdoor activities

* 70 acre campus with walled garden, set in beautiful North Oxfordshire countryside

* Easy access to Stratford, Oxford, Cheltenham, Birmingham, London

Religious activities: The School is affiliated to the Religious Society of Friends (Quakers). It welcomes pupils of all faiths, backgrounds and nationalities, encouraging in each of them genuine self-esteem in a vigorous, caring and challenging environment.

Stanbridge Earls School

(Founded 1952)

*Romsey,
Hampshire SO51 0ZS
Tel: 0794 516777 Fax: 0794 511201*

Head: Mr H. Moxon, MA, DipEd
Age range: 11-18. Boarders from 11
No. of pupils enrolled as at 1.1.92: 180
Senior: 154 Boys 26 Girls; Sixth Form: 32 Boys 1 Girl
Fees per annum: Day: £2200, Boarding: £2970
Sixth Form: Day £2420, Boarding £3245

Type: Independent co-educational special learning difficulties; emotional; interrupted education; some physical problems.

Religious denomination: Church of England

Member of: SHMIS, BSA, GBA

Curriculum: All the traditional subjects are offered up to GCSE level but there is a great variety of alternatives designed to develop the strengths and interests of every pupil, such as Drama, Craft, Design and Technology, Motor Vehicle Studies, Photography. 13 subjects are available at A level. Many pupils are dyslexic but everyone takes GCSE and most achieve at least five. A number of leavers go to University, Polytechnics and other centres of Higher Education.

Entry requirements and procedures: By interview, school report and, where appropriate, educational psychologist's report.

Examinations offered: GCSE: SEG, MEG and NEA. A level: London and AEB.

Academic and leisure facilities: The School has excellent facilities for all academic subjects. There is a wide choice of games and the School has a large sports hall, indoor swimming pool, squash courts, floodlit tennis courts, and playing fields. Sailing is done from Lymington. There is a choice of 30 activities to choose from over the year.

We specialise in consultancy, design, production and publication of:

- [✓] **Prospectuses**
- [✓] **Mini-prospectuses**
- [✓] **Newsletters**
- [✓] **Exhibition Materials**
- [✓] **Marketing**
- [✓] **Video Films**
- [✓] **School Magazines**
- [✓] **School Year Books**

Our experience and quality of craftsmanship enable us to give a service which we believe is unequalled by any other organisation at a highly competitive price.

John Catt Educational Limited
Great Glemham,
Saxmundham,
Suffolk IP17 2DH
Tel: 0728 78 666   Fax: 0728 78 415

Colleges of Further Education

Beaumont College of Further Education

(Founded 1977)

*Slyne Road,
Lancaster LA2 6AP
Tel: 0524 64278 Fax: 0524 846896*

Principal: David Gilbert
(Member of British Accreditation Council and NATSPEC)
Age range: 16-19+. Residential with some non-residents
No. of pupils enrolled as at 1.1.92: 76
Fees: Day: £5000 per term
Boarding: £22,500 per annum

Type: College of Further Education

Religious denomination: Interdenominational

Member of: N.W. SEMERC (Oldham), ISAAC, BACHFE, SKILL, NATSPEC

Curriculum: The curriculum which regards students as differently able rather than disabled, is delivered by a multi-disciplinary team - Lecturers, Therapists, Student Support Workers and aims to maximise the potential of each student towards independent living. Specific skills in basic education, daily living tasks, and communication are developed. Opportunities for leisure and creative interests (dance, drama, sound, video work etc) are also offered both within the College and the wider community. Microtechnology is used to facilitate equal access to the curriculum for all students.

Coleg Elidyr

(Founded 1973)

*Rhandirmwyn,
Nr Llandovery,
Dyfed SA20 0NL
Tel: 05506 272 Fax: 05506 331*

Head: Miss L.M. Dent
Age range: 16+
No. of pupils enrolled as at 1.1.92:
100 young men and women
Fees per annum: Boarding: £9000

Type: Further Educational College for school leavers with Special Educational Needs.

Religious denomination: Inter-denominational

Member of: NCSE, SKILL, Association of Camphill Communities (Rudolf Steiner)

Curriculum: Three Year Course including subject teaching, eurythmy, music, folk dancing, drama, speech, gym and games. Broad range of craft activities. Wide variety of work experience in teams including farming (dairy, sheep, poultry), gardening and estate work, forestry, shop-keeping, cooking and baking, laundry/domestic work, guest house management, swimming, hiking, camping.

Apprenticeships: Some students stay on for further period after Three Year Course. Choice includes farming, gardening, guest house management etc., and at apprentice houses in Llangadog, weaving, woodwork, cooking, baking and serving in Coleg's cafe.

Glasallt Fawr Farm: where journeymen can use their skills.

Useful Associations

Advisory Centre for Education (ACE) Ltd

1B Aberdeen Studios
22-24 Highbury Grove
London N5 2EA

Tel: 071 354 8321

Association of Blind and Partially-Sighted Teachers and Students

5 Gravel Hill
Tile Hill
Coventry CV4 9JD

Tel: 0203 468899

Secretary: Elizabeth Standen

Association for Brain-Damaged Children

Clifton House
3 St Paul's Road
Foleshill
Coventry CV6 5DE

Tel: 0203 665450

Association of Educational Psychologists

3 Sunderland Road
Durham
DH1 2LH

Tel: 091 384 9512

Secretary: Ms A. Baumber, BSc, MEd

The Association for the Education and Welfare of the Visually Handicapped

School of Education
University of Birmingham
PO Box 363
Birmingham B15 2TT

Tel: 021 414 4799

Hon Secretary: Mrs J.M. Stone

Association of National Specialist Colleges (NATSPEC)

c/o Lord Mayor Treloar College
Holybourne
Alton
Hants GU34 4EN

Tel: 0420 83508

Hon Secretary: Dr J. Lones

Association of Professions for Mentally Handicapped People

Greytree Lodge
Second Avenue
Ross-on-Wye
Herefordshire HR9 7HT

Tel: 0989 62630

Secretary: Mrs J. Woolf

Promotes general welfare of people with learning difficulties and their families.

Association of Speech Impaired Children (AFASIC)

347 Central Market
Smithfield
London EC1A 9NH

Tel: 071 236 3632

Supports and advises parents and professionals.

Association for Spinabifida and Hydrocephalus

42 Park Road
Peterborough PE1 2UQ

Tel: 0733 555988
Fax: 0733 555985

Executive Director: Miss Moyna P. Gilbertson, MCSP, FBIM

Association of Workers for Maladjusted Children

Red Hill School
Carlton Court
East Sutton
Maidstone
Kent ME17 3DQ

General Secretary: Allan Rimmer

British Association of Teachers of the Deaf (BATOD)

Icknield High School HIU
Riddy Lane
Luton
Bedfordshire
LU3 2AH

Tel: 0582 596599

Secretary: S.P. Dowe

The association represents the interests of all teachers of the hearing-impaired in this country.

British Deaf Association

38 Victoria Place
Carlisle
CA1 1HU

Tel: 0228 48844

Aims to advance and promote the interests of the deaf. Education dept organises adventure holidays.

British Dyslexia Association

98 London Road
Reading
Berkshire
RG1 5AU

Tel: 0734 668271

British Dyslexia Trust

39 Portman Square
London W1H 9HB

Tel: 071 722 8739

Sister organisation to BDA. Set up in 1984 to generate funds for teacher training courses to overcome dyslexia.

British Epilepsy Association

Anstey House
40 Hanover Square
Leeds
LS3 1BE

Tel: 0532 439393

British Institute for Brain-Damaged Children

Knowle Hall
Knowle
Bridgwater
Somerset

Tel: 0278 684060

Promotes a specific form of therapy which stimulates the nervous system.

BIMH
British Institute of Mental Handicap

Wolverhampton Road
Kidderminster
Worcestershire DY10 3PP

Tel: 0562 850251

BIMH works towards improving the quality of life of people with learning difficulties.

British Psychological Society

48 Princess Road East
Leicester LE1 7DR

Tel: 0533 549 568

The Cambridge Specific Learning Disabilities Group

Department of Education
University of Cambridge
5 Benet Place
Cambridge CB2 1EL

Tel: 0223 356903

Chairman: Dr D. Bruce
Secretary: Mrs B. Wattles

Centre for Studies on Integration in Education (CSIE)

4th Floor
415 Edgeware Road
London NW2 6NB

Tel: 081 452 8642

Advice and publications for parents wishing their children with special needs to be integrated into mainstream schools.

Child Psychotherapy Trust

27 Ulysses Road
London NW6 1ED

Children's Aid Team

75-77 Granville Road
London N22

Tel: 081 888 4189

Support Service for children with learning difficulties and their families.

Children's Legal Centre

20 Compton Terrace
London N1 2UN

Tel: 071 359 6251

College of Speech Therapists

Harold Poster House
6 Lechmere Road
London NW2 5BU

Tel: 081 459 8521

Conductive Education Association (CEA)

7 West End Avenue
Pinner
Middlesex HA5 1BN

Tel: 081 866 0425

Aims to promote the knowledge and practice of conductive education.

Cystic Fibrosis Research Trust

Alexandra House
5 Blyth Road
Bromley
Kent
BR1 3RS

Tel: 081 464 7211

Down's Syndrome Association

153-155 Mitcham Road
London SW17 9PG

Tel: 071 682 4012

Dyslexia Institute

133 Gresham Road
Staines
Middlesex
TW18 2JX

Tel: 0784 59498

Director of Studies: Dr H.T. Chasty
Administration Director: Mrs E.J. Brooks

Foundation for Conductive Education

University of Birmingham
PO Box 363
Birmingham
B15 2TT

Tel: 021 414 4947

Formed in 1986 to establish conductive education in the UK.

Hornsey Trust for Handicapped Children

26A Dukes Avenue
London N10 2PT

Tel: 081 444 7242

Provides education based on conductive ideas.

Independent Panel for Special Education Advice

12 Marsh Road
Tillingham
Essex
CM10 7SZ

Tel: 0621 779781

Co-ordinator: John Wright

Helps parents who want a second opinion (free of charge) about the professional advice they have received regarding their children's special educational needs, and gives advice on statementing.

The Institute for Neurophysiological Psychology

4 Stanley Place
Chester
Cheshire CH1 2LU

Tel: 0244 311414

Sally Goddard - Associate of INPP

Established in 1975 to research into the effect Central Nervous System dysfunctions have on children with Learning Difficulties and adults suffering from neuroses, and to develop appropriate CNS remedial and rehabilitation programmes.

Invalid Children's Aid Nationwide (I CAN)

Allen Graham House
198 City Road
London EC1V 2PH

Tel: 071 608 2462

Director: J. McKinnon

Learning Development Aids

Duke Street
Wisbech
Cambridgeshire PE13 2AE

Tel: 0945 63441

Makaton Vocabulary Development Project

31 Firwood Drive
Camberley
Surrey GU15 3QD

Tel: 0276 61390

Makaton Vocabulary is a language programme which provides basic means of communication and encourages language to develop in children.

MIND (National Association for Mental Health)

22 Harley Street
London W1N 2ED

Tel: 071 637 0741

National Director: Ros Hepplewhite

National Association for Gifted Children

Park Campus
Boughton Green Road
Northampton NN2 7AL

Tel: 0604 792300

Director: M. Short

National Association for Remedial Teaching

2 Lichfield Road
Stafford ST17 4JX

Tel: 0785 46872

Hon Secretary: Ms D. Smith

National Association of Independent and Non-maintained Special Schools (NAIMS)

c/o St Mary's School
Wrestwood Road, Bexhill-on-Sea
East Sussex TN40 2LU

Tel: 0424 730740

Secretary: Miss J. Shaw

NARE
National Association for Remedial Education

Central Office, 2 Lichfield Road
Stafford ST17 4JX

Tel: 0785 46872
Fax: 0785 41187

The Association is concerned with the prevention, investigation, and treatment of learning difficulties from whatever source they may emanate and which hinder the educational development of the student.

The National Autistic Society

276 Willesden Lane
London NW2 5RB

Tel: 081 451 1114
Fax: 081 451 5865

The National Autistic Society offers families and carers information, advice and support.

National Children's Bureau (NCB)

8 Wakley Street
London EC1V 7QE

Tel: 071 278 9441

National Council for Special Education

1 Wood Street
Stratford-upon-Avon CV37 2JE

Tel: 0789 205332

Secretary: J. Garrett, OBE

National Deaf Children's Society

NDCS Family Services Centre
Carlton House
24 Wakefield Road
Rothwell Haigh
Leeds LS26 0SF

0532 823458 (voice and text)
0532 824113 (fax)
0800 252380 (parents freefone 1-5 weekdays)

Advice is available on all aspects of deaf children's education and welfare, including personal help with reviews and appeals. Full information service with lending library and research collection.

NDCS Technology Information Centre

4 Church Road
Edgbaston
Birmingham B15 3TD

021 454 5151 (voice and text)
021 454 5044 (fax)
0800 424 545 (parents freefone 1-5 weekdays)

Advice and information on equipment and technology for deaf children at home and at school.

NDCS National Office

45 Hereford Road
London W2 5AH

071 229 9272 (voice and text)
071 243 0195 (fax)

The National Office co-ordinates policy development, campaigns and public awareness. There are two departments, Administration and Finance, and Membership and Public Services which also deals with publications, services for members and for NDCS local groups. The Director is based at National Office.

The National Council for Special Education

Exhall Grange
Wheelwright Lane
Coventry CV7 9HP

Tel: 0203 362414

The National Council exists to further the education and welfare of all who are in any way disabled.

Network 81

52 Magnaville Road
Bishop's Stortford
Hertfordshire
CM23 4DW

Tel: 0279 503244

Secretary: Elizabeth Arondelle

A national network of support groups of parents of children who have special educational needs.

Network for the Handicapped

16 Princeton Street
London WC1R 4BB

Tel: 071 831 7740

Provides a broad range of free legal advice and assistance on education and many other matters specifically for disabled people, their families and friends.

Paget Gorman Signed Speech (PGSS)

3 Gipsy Lane
Headington
Oxford
OX3 7PT

Tel: 0865 61908

Advice and information for parents and professionals.

Rapid Action for Conductive Education (RACE)

155 St John's Hill
London SW11 1TQ

Rathbone Society

1st Floor
Princess House
105-107 Princess Street
Manchester M1 6DD

Tel: 061 236 5358

A national society working for and on behalf of people with learning difficulties.
Provides a wide range of services.

Research Centre for the Education of the Visually Handicapped

Faculty of Education
Dept of Special Education
Selly Wick House,
59 Selly Wick Road
Birmingham B29 7JE

Tel: 021 471 1303

Royal Association for Disability and Rehabilitation (RADAR)

25 Mortimer Street
London W1N 8AB

Tel: 071 637 5400

Information on all aspects of disability.

The Royal National Institute for the Blind (RNIB)

224 Great Portland Street
London W1N 6AA

Tel: 071 388 1266

Director General: Ian Bruce
Director of Education and Leisure: Paul Ennals

The Royal National Institute for the Deaf

105 Gower Street
London WC1E 6AH

Tel: 071 387 8033

Director: M. Whitlam

The RNID is a voluntary organisation representing the interests of deaf, deaf-blind and hard of hearing people.

Royal Society for Mentally Handicapped Children and Adults

Mencap National Centre
123 Golden Lane
London EC1Y 0RT

Tel: 071 253 9433

Director - Education, Training & Employment: F. Heddell

Scottish Council for Educational Technology

74 Victoria Crescent
Glasgow G12 9JN

Tel: 041 334 9314

Information on the use of microelectronics in special needs. Special Educational Needs Database (SEND).

Scottish Council for Spastics

Rhuemore
22 Corstorphine Road
Edinburgh
EH12 6HP

Tel: 031 337 2804

Scottish Learning Difficulties Association

53 Craw Road
Paisley
Renfrewshire
PA2 6AE

Tel: 041 889 7540

Secretary: Mrs I. White

Scottish Society for Autistic Children

24D Barony Street
Edinburgh EH3 6YY

Tel: 031 557 0474

Scottish Society for Mentally Handicapped

13 Elmbank Street
Glasgow G2 4QA

Tel: 041 226 4541

Sense
The National Deaf-Blind & Rubella Association

311 Gray's Inn Road
London WC1X 8PT

Tel: 071 278 1005
Fax: 071 837 3267

Chief Executive: Rodney Clark
Director of Education: Charles Byrne

SENNAC
Special Educational Needs - National Advisory Council

Hillside
271 Woolton Road
Liverpool

Tel: 051 722 3819

Hon Secretary: Ian Petrie

SKILL
National Bureau for Students with Disabilities

336 Brixton Road
London SW9 7AA

Tel: 071 274 0565
Fax: 071 274 7840

Director: Ms D.C. Cooper
Information Officer: Ms E. Delap

SKILL is a voluntary organisation which aims to develop opportunities for young people and adults with special needs - in further, higher and adult education, in training and employment.

Spastics Society

12 Park Crescent
London W1N 4EQ

Tel: 071 636 5020

Spastics Society Education Department

840 Brighton Road
Purley
Surrey CR2 0HW

Tel: 081 660 8552

Special Needs Advisory Project (SNAP)

169 City Road
Cardiff CF2 3JB

Tel: 0222 494933

Trains and supports volunteers to enable them to give information, support and guidance to parents on issues relating to Special Educational Provision in Mid, South and West Glamorgan, and Gwent.

Understanding Disabilities Educational Trust

Weydon School
Weydon Lane
Farnham
Surrey GU9 8UG

Tel: 0252 733167
Fax: 0252 734306

Executive Director: Ms M. Grant
Development Officer: Craig Crowley

Voluntary Council for Handicapped Children

8 Wakley Street
London EC1V 7QE

Tel: 071 278 9441

Comprehensive information about services and sources of help.

Counties and Regions of Britain

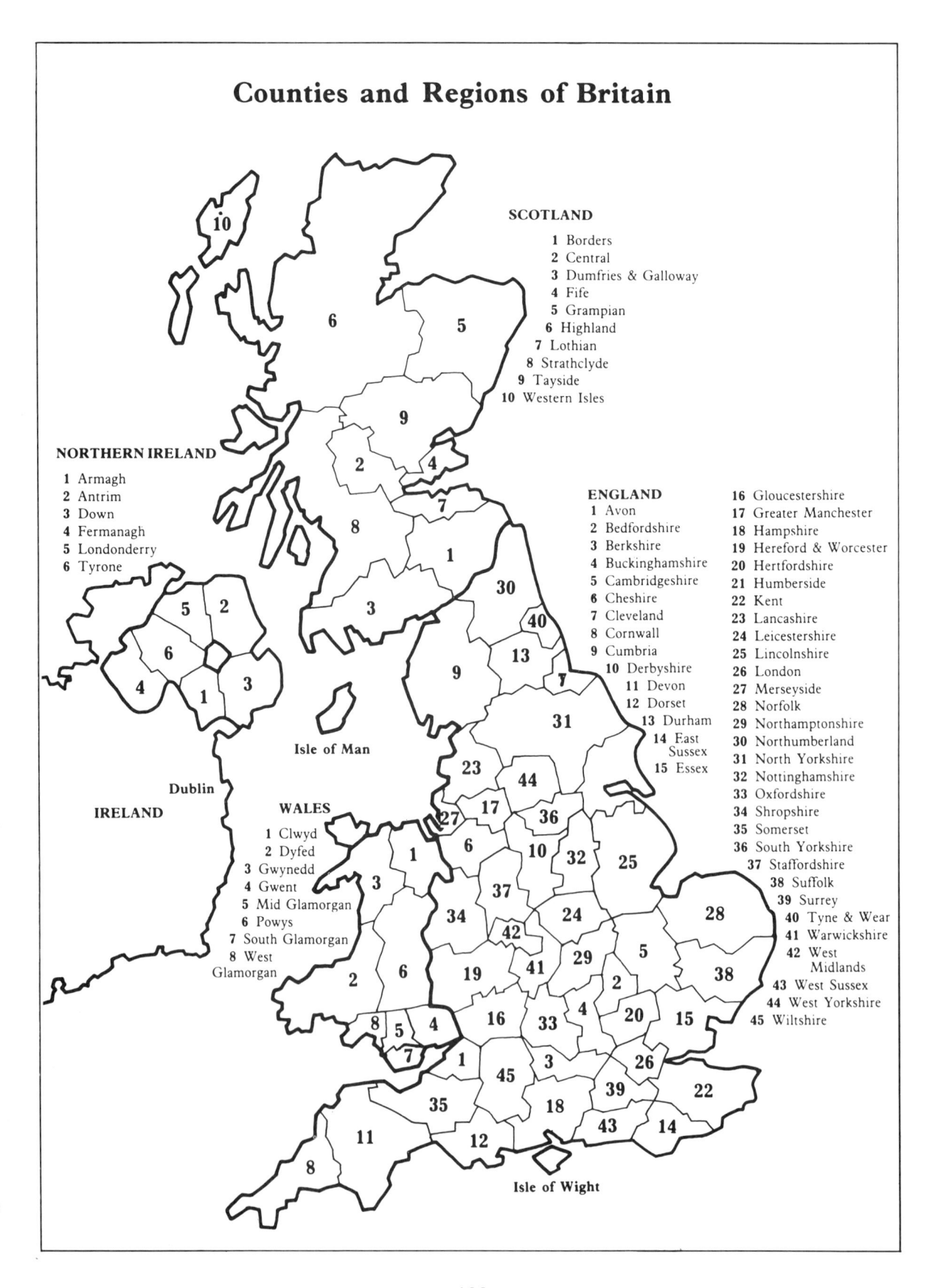

SCOTLAND
1. Borders
2. Central
3. Dumfries & Galloway
4. Fife
5. Grampian
6. Highland
7. Lothian
8. Strathclyde
9. Tayside
10. Western Isles

NORTHERN IRELAND
1. Armagh
2. Antrim
3. Down
4. Fermanagh
5. Londonderry
6. Tyrone

ENGLAND
1. Avon
2. Bedfordshire
3. Berkshire
4. Buckinghamshire
5. Cambridgeshire
6. Cheshire
7. Cleveland
8. Cornwall
9. Cumbria
10. Derbyshire
11. Devon
12. Dorset
13. Durham
14. East Sussex
15. Essex
16. Gloucestershire
17. Greater Manchester
18. Hampshire
19. Hereford & Worcester
20. Hertfordshire
21. Humberside
22. Kent
23. Lancashire
24. Leicestershire
25. Lincolnshire
26. London
27. Merseyside
28. Norfolk
29. Northamptonshire
30. Northumberland
31. North Yorkshire
32. Nottinghamshire
33. Oxfordshire
34. Shropshire
35. Somerset
36. South Yorkshire
37. Staffordshire
38. Suffolk
39. Surrey
40. Tyne & Wear
41. Warwickshire
42. West Midlands
43. West Sussex
44. West Yorkshire
45. Wiltshire

WALES
1. Clwyd
2. Dyfed
3. Gwynedd
4. Gwent
5. Mid Glamorgan
6. Powys
7. South Glamorgan
8. West Glamorgan

Isle of Man

Dublin

IRELAND

Isle of Wight

Index

A

Adlestrop Park School D86
Alderwasley Hall D28
Alexander Anderson Home D35
Allington Manor School D86
Annie Lawson School D62

B

Badgeworth Court School D86
Banstead Place Assessment & Further Education D32
Beaumont College of Further Education 120
Beech Tree School D87
Berrow Wood School D86
Besford Court School D63
Bessels Leigh School D88
Bethany School, Cranbrook 107
Bethesda School D28, 38
Birkdale School for Hearing Impaired Children D31, 38
Birtenshaw Hall School D30
Bladon House School D32
Bourne Place School D63
Boveridge House D62, 71
Bradfield House School D62
Bramfield House D89
Breckenbrough School D90
Brickwall School D67, 71
Broomhayes School D62
Broughton House School D88
Bryn Alyn Community, Clwyd 107
Burwood Park School and College D32

C

Caldecott Community School D87
Caldwell Hall D28
Camphill Blair Drummond Trust D69
Cedar House School D87
Center Academy D64, 72
Chaigeley School D84
Chailey Heritage School D33, 40
Chelfham Mill School D84
Chelfham Senior School D84
Chelmer Residential School D85
Chelmsford Hall, Eastbourne 108
Childscourt School D89
City of London School for Girls D100
Clarence House School D88
Coleg Elidyr 120
College For Deaf People (Derby) D28

Condover Hall School D32
Coney Hill School D30
Corseford School D35
Cotsbrook Community D89
Cotswold Chine Home School D86
Coxlease School D86
Craig-y-Parc School D35, 39
Crowthorn School D64, 72
Cruckton Hall School D89, 95

D

Dame Hannah Rogers School D28
Dawn House School D65, 73
Dedisham School D90
Delamere Forest School D28
Delarue College D30
Derwen College for the Disabled D32
Donaldson's School for the Deaf D35
Doncaster College for the Deaf D34
Dorton House School, Royal London Society
  for the Blind D30, 41
Doucecroft School D63
Downshead School, Seaford D94

E

East Court D63
East Park Home School D68
Eden Grove School D84
Edgarley Hall (Millfield Junior School), Glastonbury 109
Edington and Shapwick Schools, Bridgwater 110
Edington School 65
Edwardstone House School D85
Ellough School D66, 109
Extended Education Unit D68

F

Fairley House School D64, 74
Farney Close School D90, 96
Feversham School D90
Freefolk House D86
Fullerton House School D68

G

Garvald School and Training Centre D69
Grange House School D63, 74
Grangewood Hall School D85
Grateley House School D86

Great Stoney School D63
Greenwood School D85
Grenville College 111
Greystone House School D84, 97

H

Halliwick College D30, 42
Hamilton Lodge School D33
Hampstead International School D64
Harmeny School D91
Hawkhurst Court Dyslexia Centre D67, 75
Hawksworth Hall School D34, 42
Helen Allison School D63
Helen Arkell Dyslexia Centre D64
Henshaw's College D34
Hereward College of Further Education D34
Hesley Hall School D90
High Close School D99
Highdene School D84
Hilbre School D88
Hill House School D86
Hillcroft Preparatory School 112
Hilltop School & Therapeutic Community D89
Hilton Grange School D91
Hinwick Hall College of Further Education D31
Holly Bank School D34
Holly House D67
Hope Lodge School D63
Hornsey Centre for Children Learning D31
House of Falkland School D91

I

Ian Tetley Memorial School D68
Inglefield Manor School D33, 43

J

Jordanstown Schools D35

K

Keffolds Farms Tutorial School D66
Kesgrave Hall School D89
Kilworthy House D85
Kinloss School D63
Kisharon School D64
Kisimul School D64, 76

L

Langside School D29
Lendrick Muir School D68
Linn Moor Residential School D68, 76
Longdon Hall D32
Loppington House Further Education & Adult Centre D65
Lord Mayor Treloar College D29, 44

M

MacIntyre School D62, 77
Maple Hayes Dyslexia School D66, 78
Mark College D66, 78
Marland School D85
Meath School D66
Meldreth Manor School D29, 45
Merton Hall D92
Mill Hall Oral School for the Deaf D33
Moats Tye School D66
Moon Hall School 113
Moor House School D32
Mordaunt School D29
More House School D66
Mulberry Bush School D88
Muntham House School D89, 100

N

Nash House D30
National Star Centre College of Further Education D29, 58
NCH Headlands School D69
Netherton Hall School D85
New Barns School D86
Northease Manor D67
Northern Counties School for the Deaf D33
Nugent House School D87, 101
Nunnykirk Hall School D65, 79

O

Ochil Tower (Rudolf Steiner) School D91
Overley Hall School D65
Ovingdean Hall School D33, 46
Owlswick School D67
Oxley Parker School D85

P

Parayhouse School D64, 80
Parkview School D91
Penhurst School D31, 47
Percy Hedley School D33
Peterhouse School for Autistic Children D64
Philpots Manor School D90
Pield Heath School D65
Pilgrims, The National School for Asthma & Eczema D33
Pipewood School D32

Index

Pontville School D64
Port Regis School D87
Portfield School D62
Portland College D31
Potterspury Lodge School D88
Princess Margaret School D32

Q

Queen Alexandra College D34
Queen Elizabeth's Foundation for the Disabled,
 Leatherhead D32, 59
Queen Ethelburga's College 114
Queen's Park School Dyslexia Centre D65

R

Red Brae Residential School D91
Red Hill School D87
Reeves Hall School D65
Ripplevale School D87
Riverside School D84
RNIB Condover Hall School, Shrewsbury D32, 48
RNIB Hethersett College D32, 49, 60
RNIB New College D29, 49
RNIB Rushton Hall School D31, 51
RNIB Sunshine House Schools D31, D33, 52
Rochester House D29
Rowden House School D63
Rowen House School D84
Royal Blind School D35
Royal Cross Primary School D30
Royal National College for the Visually Impaired D29
Royal School for Deaf Children D30, 53
Royal School for the Deaf D28
Royal School for the Blind D31, D33
Royal School for the Deaf (Manchester) D28
Royal West of England School for the Deaf D28
Rutherfords School D67
Rutland House School D31, 53

S

Salesian School D86
Shapwick Senior School D66
Sheiling School Camphill Community, Bristol D62, 82
Sheridan House School & Family Therapy Unit D88
Shotton Hall School D89
Sibford School 117
South Lodge School D87, 103
Southlands School D87
Spinney School D90, 103
Spring Hill School D90
St Catherine's School D30
St Christophers School D62

St David's College, Llandudno 115
St Dominics School D33
St Edward's School, Romsey D87, 102
St Edwards School D87
St Elizabeth's RC School D30
St Francis School D85
St John's RC School D34
St John's Residential School D67
St Josephs School, Cranleigh D67, 81
St Luke's 16 Plus For Independent Training D85
St Luke's School D85
St Margaret's School D67
St Mary's School D33
St Piers Lingfield D67
St Rose's Special School D29, 54
St Thomas More's School D85
St Vincent's School D31, 55
Stanbridge Earls School 118
Stanmore House Residential School D35
Stonecourt School D90
Storm House School D68
Struan House School D68
Sunfield Childrens Homes D68
Sutcliffe School D90
Sutherland House School (Primary Department) D65
Sutherland House School (Secondary Department) D65
Sydney House Communities, Westgate-on-Sea D104

T

Templehill Community School D68
The Camphill Rudolf Steiner Schools D35
The Chalvington Trust School D89
The David Lewis School D62
The Grange D28
The Grange School D88
The Grange Training Centre & Sheltered Workshop D32
The Helen Allison School, Meopham D75
The House in the Sun School D87
The John Horniman School D67
The Knowl Hill School D66
The Learning Centre D88
The Link Day Primary School D66
The Link Secondary School D66
The Loddon School D86
The Manor House D30
The Marchant-Holliday School D89, 100
The Mary Hare Grammar School for the Deaf D28
The Mount Camphill Steiner School D89
The National Star Centre D29, 58
The Old Rectory School D66, 79
The Royal School for Deaf Children (Margate) D30
The Ryes School D89
The Sheiling Curative Schools D63
The Sheiling School D62, 82

Index

The St John Vianney School D62, D64
The Sybil Elgar School D64
The Victoria School D29
The West of England School D29
Tregynon Hall, Newtown 104
Trengweath School D28, 56
Tyne and Wear Autistic Society D67

U

Underley Garden School D87
Underley Hall School D88

V

Vranch House School & Hill Barton House D29, 56

W

Wargrave House School for Autistic Children D65
Warleigh School D84
West Kirby Residential School D88, 105
Westerlea School D35
Whitstone Head School D84
William Henry Smith School D91
Wilsic Hall School D91
Witherslack Hall D84
Woodcroft School D63
Woodlands School D92
Woodsford House D62

Reader Enquiry Card

For more information about schools and colleges listed in Which School ? for Special Needs 1992/3, write the name of the school(s) or college(s) that interest(s) you below:

Post this card to John Catt Educational Limited; a stamp is not necessary if posted in the UK. Brochures and information concerning the institution(s) you have requested will be sent to you as soon as possible.

YOUR NAME:

ADDRESS:

Reader Enquiry Card

For more information about schools and colleges listed in Which School ? for Special Needs 1992/3, write the name of the school(s) or college(s) that interest(s) you below:

Post this card to John Catt Educational Limited; a stamp is not necessary if posted in the UK. Brochures and information concerning the institution(s) you have requested will be sent to you as soon as possible.

YOUR NAME:

ADDRESS:

Reader Enquiry Card

For more information about schools and colleges listed in Which School ? for Special Needs 1992/3, write the name of the school(s) or college(s) that interest(s) you below:

Post this card to John Catt Educational Limited; a stamp is not necessary if posted in the UK. Brochures and information concerning the institution(s) you have requested will be sent to you as soon as possible.

YOUR NAME:

ADDRESS:

Reader Enquiry Card

For more information about schools and colleges listed in Which School ? for Special Needs 1992/3, write the name of the school(s) or college(s) that interest(s) you below:

Post this card to John Catt Educational Limited; a stamp is not necessary if posted in the UK. Brochures and information concerning the institution(s) you have requested will be sent to you as soon as possible.

YOUR NAME:

ADDRESS:

BUSINESS REPLY SERVICE
Licence No. WD 598

John Catt Educational Ltd

Great Glemham
Saxmundham
Suffolk
IP17 2DH

BUSINESS REPLY SERVICE
Licence No. WD 598

John Catt Educational Ltd

Great Glemham
Saxmundham
Suffolk
IP17 2DH

BUSINESS REPLY SERVICE
Licence No. WD 598

John Catt Educational Ltd

Great Glemham
Saxmundham
Suffolk
IP17 2DH

BUSINESS REPLY SERVICE
Licence No. WD 598

John Catt Educational Ltd

Great Glemham
Saxmundham
Suffolk
IP17 2DH